ANNE WILLAN'S
LOOK&COOK

Splendid Soups

ANNE WILLAN'S
LOOK&COOK

Splendid Soups

DORLING KINDERSLEY
LONDON • NEW YORK • STUTTGART

A DORLING KINDERSLEY BOOK

Created and Produced by
CARROLL & BROWN LIMITED
5 Lonsdale Road
London NW6 6RA

Editorial Director Jeni Wright
Editorial Consultant Norma MacMillan
Editors Anne Crane
Anna Brandenburger

Managing Art Editor Lyndel Donaldson
Art Editor Alan Watt
Designers Lucy De Rosa
Carmel O'Neill
Production Editor Wendy Rogers

First published in Great Britain in 1994
by Dorling Kindersley Limited
9 Henrietta Street, London WC2E 8PS

A CIP catalogue record for this book is available
from the British Library
ISBN 0-7513-0068-3

Reproduced by Colourscan, Singapore
Printed and bound in Italy by A. Mondadori, Verona

CONTENTS

SOUPS

THE LOOK & COOK APPROACH

INGREDIENTS

Welcome to **Splendid Soups** and the *Look & Cook* series. These volumes are designed to be the simplest, most informative cookbooks you'll ever own. They are the closest I can come to sharing my techniques for cooking my own favourite recipes without actually being with you in the kitchen.

Equipment and ingredients often determine whether or not you can cook a particular dish, so *Look & Cook* illustrates everything you need at the beginning of each recipe. You'll see at a glance how long a recipe takes to cook, how many servings it makes, what the finished dish looks like, and how much preparation can be done ahead. When you start to cook, you'll find the preparation and cooking are organized into easy-to-follow steps. Each stage has its own colour coding and everything is shown in photographs with brief text for each step. You will never be in doubt as to what it is you are doing, why you are doing it, and how it should look.

🍽 SERVES 4-6   ⏳ WORK TIME 25-35 MINUTES   🍲 COOKING TIME 20-30 MINUTES

I've also included helpful hints and ideas under "Anne Says". These may list an alternative ingredient or piece of equipment, or explain a certain method, or offer some advice on mastering a particular technique. Similarly, if there is a crucial stage in a recipe when things can go wrong, I've included some warnings called "Take Care".

Many of the photographs are annotated to pinpoint why certain pieces of equipment work best, or how food should look at the various stages of cooking. Because presentation is so important, there is a picture of the finished dish with serving suggestions at the end of each recipe.

Thanks to all this information, you can't go wrong. I'll be with you every step of the way. So please come with me into the kitchen to look, cook, and create some **Splendid Soups**.

WHY SOUPS?

A soup can be warmly sustaining in winter, or thirst-quenching on a hot day. It can be piquant and arresting, or hearty and satisfying. Soup can begin a meal, helping to balance simple fare such as pasta or a sandwich, or whetting the appetite for a succulent main-course dish – or it can be a meal in itself, needing only bread as an accompaniment to make it satisfying. Soup can be made from humble ingredients – root vegetables and dried beans, older and tougher birds, and cuts of meat – or from grand ones, such as shellfish, wine, and cream.

RECIPE CHOICE

You may be surprised by the variety of soup recipes in this volume. The selection includes elegant clear broths, smooth creamed purées, hearty and filling soups, and refreshing cold soups. Influences come from many cuisines, including those of Asia, India, the Middle East, Eastern and Western Europe, Latin America, and the North American continent. From this collection you can be sure to find a soup for every occasion and every season.

CLEAR SOUPS

Light Vegetable Broth with Parmesan Dumplings: an aromatic broth with colourful, crisp vegetables and fresh herbs is finished with tiny cheese dumplings. *Light Vegetable Broth with Cucumber:* a delicate vegetable broth is given green freshness with slices of cucumber and fine shreds of lettuce. *French Onion Soup (Soupe à l'Oignon)*: rich beef stock and red wine provide the backbone for a hearty onion soup served with traditional Gruyère cheese-topped croûtes. *Sweet Onion Soup with Shallots*: the sweet flavour of onions is enhanced by a spoonful of hot spicy Dijon mustard and chopped fresh tarragon.

Mushroom and Wild Rice Soup: dried wild mushrooms and button mushrooms, juniper berries, and port wine give a pungent flavour to this rich soup. *Thai Hot and Sour Prawn Soup (Tom Yung Gung)*: sweet juicy prawns blend well with hot chilli and sour citrus flavours in a typical Thai soup. *Hot and Sour Fish Soup*: Japanese seaweed "nori" adds an extra flavour of the sea to an aromatic white fish soup. *Chinese Greens and Wonton Soup*: gai choi and decoratively folded wontons, filled with pork, cloud ears, and ginger, float in a broth flavoured with rice wine, soy sauce, and sesame oil. *Mushroom Wonton Soup*: here wontons have a garlic-flavoured mushroom filling and the rich mushroom broth is finished with Parma ham. *Chicken Consommé with Madeira and Tomato*: rich chicken stock is the base for this classic clear soup, served with crisp Melba toast. *Chicken Consommé with Orange*: citrus adds an aromatic tang to an elegant clear soup. *Vegetable and Noodle Soup*: many vegetables – including leeks, courgettes, tomatoes, and French beans – combine with vermicelli in a rich broth.

CREAMED AND PUREED SOUPS

Cream of Mushroom and Rice Soup: a perennial favourite – cream of mushroom soup is thickened with rice and finished with fresh chives. *Spiced Carrot and Orange Soup*: fresh orange juice and ground coriander enhance the sweet flavour of carrots in this smooth soup. *Spiced Carrot and Parsnip Soup*: carrots and parsnips complement each other here, with a warm spicing of ground cumin. *Cheddar and Vegetable Soup*: an irresistible cream of vegetable soup is enriched with mature cheese and topped with crisp bacon. *Blue Cheese and Celeriac Soup*: this creamy soup is pepped up with a little dry white wine and full-flavoured blue cheese. *Fresh Green Pea Soup with Mint*: sweet peas, lettuce, fresh mint, and cream make a perfect combination. The soup is served with buttery, walnut-topped Parmesan wafers. *Fresh Green Pea Soup with Tarragon*: fresh tarragon gives an unusual and delicious flavour to creamy green soup. *Butternut Squash and Apple Soup*: fresh ginger and garlic accent this golden-hued soup, with curry-spiced croûtons to add crunch.

Pumpkin and Apple Soup: a mild spicing of curry goes well with pumpkin and apple in this harvest-time recipe. *Curried Courgette Soup*: a light, creamed summer soup with a touch of spice, garnished with fried herb croûtons. *Red Pepper Soup with Coriander Pesto*: roasted sweet peppers make a brilliant red, delicately flavoured soup – a striking contrast to the garnish of fresh herb pesto. *Golden Pepper Soup with Basil Pesto*: roasted yellow pepper soup provides a beautiful backdrop for the rich green of the pesto garnish. *Peppery Green Soup*: zesty greens give a rich colour to this soup, which is topped with cream and toasted almonds. *Peppery Green Soup with Chorizo:* spicy sausage combines well with a blend of spinach, rocket, and watercress. *Roasted Aubergine Soup with Chilli Cream*: roasted aubergines, shallots, and garlic give a sweet, smoky flavour to this unusual soup. It is finished with a spicy red chilli pepper cream and served with sesame-seed pastry twists. *Roasted Provençal Vegetable Soup*: here, courgettes, aubergines, peppers, and other vegetables from Provence are roasted and then puréed together. *American Red Bean Soup*: satisfying enough for a main dish, this bean, vegetable, and smoked bacon soup from the Southwest of the United States is accompanied by yellow cornbread sticks. *Senate Black Bean Soup*: sour cream and lemon slices top this American classic.

HEARTY SOUPS

German Split Pea Soup: a winning combination of yellow split peas, lots of vegetables, and frankfurters in a beer- and mustard-flavoured broth. *Green Split Pea and Bacon Soup*: cubes of bacon and a spicing of coriander and cloves turn split pea soup into something special. *Turkish Meatball Soup*: a rich egg-thickened broth is sharpened with lemon juice to make a pleasing contrast to lamb meatballs spiced with ground cinnamon and

allspice. *Egg and Lemon Soup with Courgettes*: rice and crisp sticks of courgette add texture here, with fresh herbs for colour and flavour. *Hearty Bean and Vegetable Soup*: haricots and fresh French beans are combined with root vegetables, cabbage, and salt pork in this garlicky peasant-style soup. Toasted French bread, spread with sun-dried-tomato butter, is a delightful accompaniment. *Monkfish and Garlic Soup with Saffron*: garlic mayonnaise adds pungency and richness to this fish soup – in the French style, it is served with extra mayonnaise and crisp croûtes. *Monkfish, Tomato, and Garlic Soup*: a tomato-garlic mayonnaise gives this soup a complex flavour and tints the broth a pale pink. *Chicken and Smoked Ham Gumbo*: this spicy soup-stew from southwest Louisiana is thickened with the sticky juices of okra. *Chicken and Prawn Gumbo:* this hearty gumbo is flavoured with Jamaican allspice, giving it an exotic Caribbean touch.

COLD SOUPS

Iced Cucumber Soup with Yogurt and Mint: refreshingly tart, this chilled soup is based on "cacik", a popular Middle Eastern salad. *Chilled Spinach and Yogurt Soup*: fresh spinach leaves, garlic, and lemon juice give depth of flavour to this smooth, creamy soup. *Chilled Guacamole Soup*: inspired by the popular Mexican avocado dip, this hot-weather soup is spiked with lime juice, tequila, and a dash of Tabasco sauce, and served with crunchy cheese-chilli tortilla chips. *Chilled Avocado Soup*: pale green and beautifully smooth, this refreshing soup is garnished with small cubes of avocado. *Gazpacho*: sun-ripened tomatoes and red peppers are the hallmarks of this Spanish classic. *Green Gazpacho with Crab*: sweet white crabmeat and black olives adorn an unusual cold soup made from spring onions, cucumber, green peppers, and herbs. *Vichyssoise*: in this soup, leeks and potatoes, two of the most humble vegetables, are transformed into the most elegant of chilled creamed soups. *Chilled Fennel, Leek, and Potato Soup*: the liquorice taste of fennel blends well with leeks and potatoes in this subtly flavoured soup. *Chilled Hungarian Cherry Soup*: this creamy tart-sweet soup, based on fresh dark sweet cherries and fruity white wine, can also be served as a summer dessert if you add a little more sugar. *Chilled Raspberry and Peach Soup*: orange and lemon juices, dry white wine, and fresh fruit purée are combined to make this delightful first-course soup.

EQUIPMENT

Most soups can be made with just a few standard kitchen utensils. A sharp chef's knife and chopping board are, of course, essential for chopping vegetables and other ingredients. In addition, you may need a small knife for trimming and peeling, plus a flexible, thin-bladed filleting knife for preparing fish and a serrated knife for bread. A cleaver makes it easy to cut up bones for stock. Other basic tools include a vegetable peeler, a grater, and a lemon squeezer. You will need a canelle knife to cut decorative vegetable shapes, and a melon baller and cherry stoner are also useful. A wooden spoon is called for in almost every recipe for stirring.

A slotted spoon and a large metal spoon are very useful, as is a ladle for transferring soup to serving bowls. For creamed soups, a rubber spatula is vital for scraping all the mixture from the side of the blender or food processor. Sometimes a puréed soup also needs to be worked through a fine-mesh sieve with a wooden spoon to remove all vegetable skins, seeds, or fibrous strings that would spoil the finished texture.

Hot soups can be made in a large saucepan, sometimes with a lid; stocks also require a large saucepan. Other pans occasionally needed are smaller saucepans, a frying pan, and a roasting tin. Most of the cooking is done on top of the stove, with the oven and grill used for accompaniments, such as Melba toast, croûtons, and wafers. You'll require a pastry brush for brushing on oil or egg glaze, and a wire rack is handy for cooling baked items.

Other equipment is on hand in most kitchens: bowls, a colander, paper towels, greaseproof paper, aluminium foil, plastic bags, baking sheets, kitchen scissors, string, ice-cube trays, and rubber gloves for handling hot chillies.

INGREDIENTS

The range of ingredients you can transform into soup is virtually endless. Most soups contain vegetables, including at least one member of the onion family, such as onions, shallots, spring onions, garlic, or leeks. You may also find roots, such as potatoes, celeriac, carrots, and turnips, or leafy greens, such as spinach, watercress, rocket, and mustard greens, plus representatives of the cabbage family, including broccoli. Don't forget the fruiting vegetables, such as aubergines, peppers, cucumbers, and courgettes. Legumes, such as dried and fresh peas and beans, are invaluable for making soup. Pasta or rice can also add body.

The heart of many good soups is homemade stock, based on meat or poultry bones for beef or chicken stock (a mature stewing chicken gives the best flavour), fish bones and heads for fish stock, or fresh vegetables for vegetable stock. More hearty soups often contain fish, shellfish, poultry, or meat as well. As an alternative to stock, wine, beer, fruit or vegetable juices, and dairy products, including buttermilk, yogurt, and cream can be used. For flavour and zest, look towards citrus juices and vinegar, and spirits and fortified wines, such as Madeira and port wine, are common.

Spices, such as cumin, and aromatic fresh herbs, such as mint and basil, can accent the underlying character of a soup. Even the old standby, parsley, is useful. The spread of Asian ingredients has widened the flavouring palate beyond Worcestershire sauce and Tabasco to include fresh ginger root, soy, lemon grass, and lime leaves. Don't hesitate to experiment with them when you have the chance.

TECHNIQUES

Puréed and creamed soups are made easy with the use of food processors and blenders. A food processor produces a purée with an even, slightly textured consistency. It is not suitable for soups containing a lot of starchy vegetables, especially potatoes, because they turn into a gluey pulp. A blender yields a smoother purée, and also emulsifies and somewhat thickens the soup, but it will not break down firm-textured ingredients unless they are thoroughly cooked. Hand blenders make quick work of puréeing soups right in the saucepan but cannot deal easily with large quantities, and the ingredients to be puréed must be soft. None of these machines will cut fibre, so soups containing tomatoes or celery must be pressed through a sieve after puréeing.

Do not overfill a food processor or blender – the finished soup will be smoother if worked in small quantities. Scrape down the side of the container with a rubber spatula so the ingredients are evenly worked. When ingredients for puréeing include a generous amount of liquid, pour out and reserve some of it. Work the solid ingredients with a little liquid, transferring them to a bowl or saucepan. Finally, stir in the amount of liquid needed to give the soup the right consistency – an easy way to control thickness and texture.

While puréeing is currently the most popular way to thicken soups, classically they are often thickened by making a butter and flour roux at the start of the recipe. The soup is then finished, just before serving, either with cream or a combination of cream and egg, called a liaison. *Crème* describes the former and *velouté* the latter style of soup.

LIGHT VEGETABLE BROTH WITH PARMESAN DUMPLINGS

 SERVES 6–8   WORK TIME 40–50 MINUTES   COOKING TIME 10 MINUTES

EQUIPMENT

chef's knife

canelle knife

ladle

food processor †

slotted spoon

wooden spoon

colander

bowls

small knife

vegetable peeler

paper towels

saucepans

chopping board

† blender can also be used

INGREDIENTS

fresh basil

fennel

mustard powder

carrots

tomatoes

celery

Parmesan cheese

flat-leaf parsley

egg

leek

vegetable stock

white bread

Aromatic with fresh vegetables and herbs, this broth is based on a delicate homemade vegetable stock. Tiny poached dumplings, made from Parmesan and breadcrumbs, are added at the last minute.

GETTING AHEAD

The vegetable stock can be prepared up to 3 days ahead; keep it, covered, in the refrigerator. For the best fresh flavour and colour, make the soup just before serving.

metric	SHOPPING LIST	imperial
1	medium leek, weighing about 175 g (6 oz)	1
3–4	small carrots, total weight about 250 g (8 oz)	3–4
2	celery sticks	2
1	small fennel bulb, weighing about 250 g (8 oz)	1
2–3	sprigs of fresh basil	2–3
2–3	sprigs of flat-leaf parsley	2–3
500 g	tomatoes	1 lb
1.5 litres	vegetable stock (see box, page 124)	2⅓ pints
	salt and pepper	
	For the Parmesan dumplings	
2	slices of white bread	2
1	egg	1
30 ml	freshly grated Parmesan cheese	2 tbsp
1	pinch of mustard powder	1

ORDER OF WORK

1 PREPARE THE VEGETABLES AND HERBS AND MAKE THE SOUP

2 MAKE THE PARMESAN DUMPLINGS AND FINISH THE SOUP

1 PREPARE THE VEGETABLES AND HERBS AND MAKE THE SOUP

1 Trim the leek, discarding the root and the tough green top. Slit the leek lengthwise in half.

2 Place each leek half, cut-side down, on the chopping board, and cut crosswise into 3 mm (⅛ inch) slices. Put the slices into a colander, wash them under cold running water, and drain.

Leeks will cook quickly when thinly sliced

Sliced carrots look like small flowers

3 Peel and trim the carrots. Run the canelle knife down the sides of the carrots to cut grooves, 5 mm (¼ inch) apart. Slice very thinly.

4 Trim the celery sticks, then peel the strings with the vegetable peeler. Using the chef's knife, cut the celery across into very thin slices.

7 Chop the basil and parsley (see box, page 12). Reserve the chopped leaves for garnish.

ANNE SAYS
"Add the herb stalks to the vegetable stock for more flavour, if you like."

5 With the chef's knife, trim the stalks and root end of the fennel bulb, discarding any tough outer pieces from the bulb.

6 Cut the fennel bulb lengthwise into quarters. Set each quarter flat on the chopping board and cut across into thin slices.

HOW TO CHOP HERBS

Basil, parsley, dill, chives, and tarragon are herbs that are usually chopped before being added to other ingredients. Do not chop delicate herbs like basil too finely because they bruise easily.

1 Strip the leaves or sprigs from the stalks and pile them on a chopping board.

Chop basil leaves coarsely to avoid bruising them

2 With a chef's knife, cut the herbs into small pieces. Holding the tip of the blade against the board, rock the knife back and forth, until the herbs are coarsely or finely chopped.

ANNE SAYS

"Make sure that your knife is very sharp, otherwise you will bruise the herbs rather than cut them."

Tomatoes are cooled in cold water before peeling

Skins slip off easily after tomatoes are scalded in boiling water

8 Core the tomatoes and score an "x" on the base of each. Immerse in boiling water until the skins split, 8–15 seconds. Transfer at once to cold water. When cool, peel, then halve crosswise. Squeeze out the seeds and chop coarsely.

9 Bring the stock to a boil in a large saucepan. Add the sliced leek, carrots, celery, and fennel. Season to taste and simmer until the vegetables are almost tender, 5–7 minutes.

10 Stir in the chopped tomatoes and simmer the vegetables, 2 minutes longer. Remove the soup from the heat; taste again for seasoning and adjust if necessary.

2 MAKE THE PARMESAN DUMPLINGS AND FINISH THE SOUP

1 Trim and discard the crusts from the bread. Cut into chunks and work in a food processor to form crumbs. You will need 75 ml (5 tbsp).

2 In a small bowl, beat the egg to mix. In another bowl, combine the breadcrumbs, Parmesan cheese, mustard powder, salt, and pepper.

3 Using a fork, gradually stir the beaten egg into the cheese mixture, adding just enough to bind the mixture together.

ANNE SAYS
"Add the egg a little at a time because it may not all be needed."

4 Bring a large saucepan of water to a simmer. Using 2 teaspoons, drop small balls of the Parmesan mixture into the simmering water and poach, 1–2 minutes, or until the dumplings are puffed up and just firm. Poach the dumplings in batches so that the pan is not crowded.

5 Remove the dumplings from the saucepan with the slotted spoon and drain on paper towels.

¶◎¶ TO SERVE
Reheat the soup, then taste for seasoning. Ladle into warmed individual bowls, add the dumplings, and serve hot, sprinkled with the reserved chopped herbs. Serve at once.

Parmesan dumplings
add lively flavour

Sliced vegetables
show clearly through light vegetable broth

LIGHT VEGETABLE BROTH WITH CUCUMBER

Thin slices of cucumber and shreds of lettuce add a fresh note to the light vegetable broth.

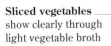

1 Omit the Parmesan dumplings. Prepare the vegetables as directed.
2 With a vegetable peeler, peel $1/2$ small cucumber (weighing about 125 g/4 oz) and cut it lengthwise in half. Using a melon baller or a teaspoon, scoop out the seeds from each half. Put each half, cut-side down, on the chopping board, and cut across into thin slices.
3 Strip the basil and parsley leaves from the stalks and tear the leaves into pieces with your fingers.
4 Rinse 3–4 leaves of round lettuce and pat dry with paper towels. Stack the leaves and roll them up loosely, then cut across the roll to make shreds.
5 Make the soup as directed, adding the cucumber slices with the tomatoes. Ladle the soup into warmed plates and sprinkle with the shredded lettuce and herbs. Serve at once.

FRENCH ONION SOUP

Soupe à l'Oignon

EQUIPMENT

- small knife
- kitchen scissors
- large pan, with lid
- chef's knife
- pastry brush
- grater
- ladle
- wooden spoon
- saucepan
- greaseproof paper
- serrated knife
- 6 heatproof soup bowls
- baking sheet

- chopping board

INGREDIENTS

- Spanish onions
- Gruyère cheese
- French baguette
- beef stock
- butter
- sugar
- red wine

This most classic of French soups was the early morning pick-me-up for the workers at Les Halles, the legendary food market, which used to be in central Paris. The soup was no doubt fortified with a good shot of Cognac. In this version, good beef stock and red wine provide the soup's backbone, and it is topped with crisp slices of French bread and grated Gruyère cheese.

GETTING AHEAD

The onion soup and croûtes can be made up to 2 days ahead. Keep the soup, covered, in the refrigerator and the croûtes in an airtight container. Reheat the soup on top of the stove, add the croûtes, and grill just before serving.

metric	SHOPPING LIST	imperial
1 kg	large Spanish onions	2 lb
60 g	butter, more for greaseproof paper	2 oz
	salt and pepper	
1.5 litres	beef stock (see box, page 124)	2⅓ pints
10 ml	sugar	2 tsp
250 ml	red wine	8 fl oz
For the topping		
1	small French baguette, weighing 175–250 g (6–8 oz)	1
30 g	butter	1 oz
90 g	Gruyère cheese	3 oz

ORDER OF WORK

1. **MAKE THE ONION SOUP**

2. **PREPARE THE TOPPING**

3. **FINISH THE SOUP**

1 MAKE THE ONION SOUP

1 Peel the onions and trim the tops, leaving a little of the root to hold the onion together.

Large Spanish onions are essential for onion soup because they have most flavour

Leave a little root to hold onion together for slicing

2 Using the chef's knife, cut the onions lengthwise in half through the root and stalk.

3 Place each half cut-side down and cut across into thin slices. Cut a piece of greaseproof paper into a round to fit the large pan.

4 Melt the butter in the large pan. Add the sliced onions and season with salt and pepper. Butter the paper and press it, buttered-side down, onto the onions.

5 Cover the pan and cook over low heat, stirring occasionally, until the onions are very soft, 20–30 minutes.

ANNE SAYS
"The onions should cook very slowly in their own juices without browning."

Stock will reduce when boiled

Flavour and colour of stock will deepen with boiling

6 Meanwhile, to concentrate the flavour of the stock, pour it into the saucepan and bring to a boil. Boil until it is reduced by one-third, 20–30 minutes.

When thoroughly browned, onions develop sweet caramel flavour

7 Remove the lid and paper from the onions and sprinkle them with the sugar.

8 Cook over medium heat, stirring occasionally, until the onions are caramelized to a golden brown, 10–15 minutes. Do not let them burn or the soup will taste bitter.

After long cooking, onions lose much of their volume

9 Add the reduced stock and the wine to the onions and bring to a boil. Partially cover the pan and simmer, 30 minutes. Meanwhile, prepare the topping for the soup.

ANNE SAYS
"Deeply caramelized onions blend with the stock and wine to give this soup its full flavour. They should be brown but not burnt."

2 PREPARE THE TOPPING

1 Heat the oven to 180°C (350°F, Gas 4). Cut the baguette diagonally into twelve slices, discarding the ends. Melt the butter. Brush the slices of bread lightly with some of the butter. Turn them over and butter the other side.

Use pastry brush for light coating of butter

2 Spread the slices of bread on the baking sheet and bake them in the heated oven until they are dry and lightly browned, turning them over once, 7–12 minutes.

ANNE SAYS
"The butter helps the slices of bread to brown when they are baked."

3 Meanwhile, grate the Gruyère cheese using the coarsest grid of the grater.

ANNE SAYS
"When the piece of cheese becomes too small to hold, stop grating and coarsely chop it."

Grated cheese will melt on toasted croûtes

3 FINISH THE SOUP

1 Heat the grill. Ladle the onion soup into heatproof soup bowls and set them on the baking sheet.

Onion soup is served in heatproof bowls to withstand heat of grill

Deep caramel brown colour is sign of good onion soup

2 Float 2 croûtes on the surface of each serving. Sprinkle the cheese over the croûtes. Set the bowls on the baking sheet and slide under the grill, close to the heat. Grill until the cheese is golden brown, 2–3 minutes.

ANNE SAYS
"If you don't have heatproof soup bowls, grill the cheese croûtes on the baking sheet and float them on the onion soup."

¶⊙¶ TO SERVE
Place the bowls on individual plates and serve immediately.

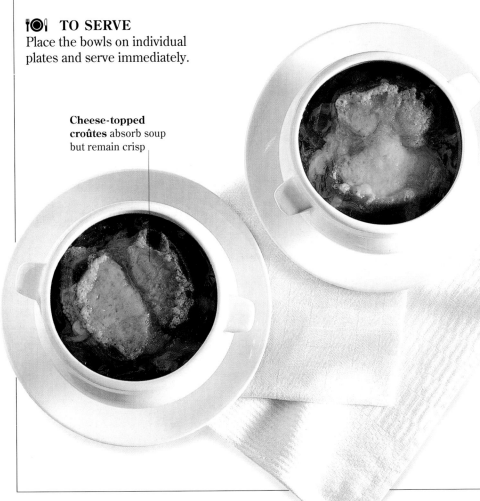

Cheese-topped croûtes absorb soup but remain crisp

V A R I A T I O N

SWEET ONION SOUP WITH SHALLOTS

Dijon mustard and fresh tarragon give an unusual flavour to this onion soup.

1 Omit the Gruyère cheese and red wine. Use 500 g (1 lb) sweet white or red-skinned onions, and peel and slice them as directed.

2 Peel 500 g (1 lb) shallots, trimming the roots, and separate into sections if necessary. Cut each whole shallot or section in half and then into quarters.

3 Melt the butter in a large pan, add the onions, shallots, salt, and pepper, and soften as directed. Remove the lid and paper from the pan, sprinkle with 15 ml (1 tbsp) sugar, and caramelize as directed.

4 Add 1.5 litres (2⅓ pints) chicken stock. Bring to a boil, half cover the pan, and simmer, about 30 minutes.

5 Meanwhile, slice, butter, and toast the bread as directed.

6 Strip the leaves from 4–6 fresh tarragon stalks and chop them.

7 Add 15 ml (1 tbsp) Dijon mustard to the soup with most of the tarragon, reserving some for garnish. Stir well. Taste for seasoning, adding more mustard, salt, and pepper if necessary.

8 Divide the slices of toasted bread among 6 warmed soup bowls and ladle in the soup. Garnish with the reserved chopped tarragon and serve at once.

THAI HOT AND SOUR PRAWN SOUP

Tom Yung Gung

EQUIPMENT

chef's knife

ladle

saucepan

small knife   rubber gloves

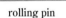
wooden spoon

rolling pin

chopping board

paper towels

The heat of green chillies and the sour tang of lemon grass and lime leaves are combined in this delicious soup, which is seasoned with Thai fish sauce or nam pla, *made by fermenting salted anchovies. Fish sauce, lemon grass, and lime leaves can all be found in Asian grocery stores.*

GETTING AHEAD
The prawns can be prepared up to 3 hours ahead and kept, tightly wrapped, in the refrigerator. Make the soup just before serving.

metric	SHOPPING LIST	imperial
500 g	raw unpeeled large prawns	1 lb
250 g	button mushrooms	8 oz
3	stalks of lemon grass	3
2	fresh hot green chillies	2
2	garlic cloves	2
9	sprigs of fresh coriander	9
1.5 litres	fish stock (see box, page 125)	2⅓ pints
5	fresh kaffir lime leaves	5
75 ml	fish sauce (nam pla)	2½ fl oz
	salt	
15 ml	lemon juice, more if needed	1 tbsp

INGREDIENTS

raw prawns   fish stock

lemon grass   button mushrooms

fresh kaffir lime leaves   fresh hot green chillies

fish sauce

lemon juice

fresh coriander   garlic cloves

ANNE SAYS
"Dried lemon grass and lime leaves can be substituted for fresh ones. Soak them in cold water, about 30 minutes, and drain before using. If you cannot obtain fresh or dried kaffir lime leaves, you can use fine strips of the thinly pared zest of 1 lime."

ORDER OF WORK

1 PREPARE THE INGREDIENTS

2 MAKE THE SOUP

1 PREPARE THE INGREDIENTS

When prawns are fresh, shells are easy to peel

Carefully pull off tail flange so prawn does not tear

1 Peel the shells from the prawns with your fingertips.

2 Make a shallow cut along the back of each prawn with the small knife and remove the dark intestinal vein.

3 If the prawns are large, place them on the chopping board and cut them lengthwise in half.

Crushing releases flavour of lemon grass

4 Clean and thinly slice the button mushrooms (see box, right). Cut off the dried leafy tops of the lemon grass, leaving 12.5–15 cm (5–6 inches) of the stalk. Peel dry outer layers until you reach the moist inner core. Cut the stalks across into 2.5 cm (1 inch) pieces. Crush them with the rolling pin.

HOW TO CLEAN AND SLICE MUSHROOMS

Mushrooms absorb moisture quickly, so do not soak them in water. In order to cook evenly, mushrooms should be cut into equal-sized pieces.

1 Wipe the mushrooms clean with damp paper towels. If necessary, rinse them in water, 1–2 seconds. Do not soak because they quickly become waterlogged.

2 With a small knife, trim the stalks just level with the caps. If using wild mushrooms, trim just the ends of the stalks.

3 To slice, hold the mushrooms stalk-side down on the chopping board and cut them vertically with a chef's knife into slices of the required thickness.

5 With the small knife, cut out the cores from the chillies. Remove the seeds with the tip of the knife. Cut each chilli across into thin rings.

ANNE SAYS
"Be sure to wear rubber gloves when preparing chillies because they can burn your skin."

For hotter soup, some chilli seeds can be included

6 Set the flat side of the chef's knife on top of each garlic clove and strike it with your fist. Discard the skin.

7 Finely chop the garlic with the chef's knife, rocking the blade back and forth.

8 Strip the coriander leaves from the stalks, reserving 6 sprigs for garnish, if you like.

Pull coriander leaves from stalks with your fingertips

2 MAKE THE SOUP

Prawns will be cooked very briefly in soup

1 Pour the stock into the saucepan, add the lemon grass and lime leaves, and bring to a boil. Simmer, 15 minutes. Stir in the fish sauce and 5 ml (1 tsp) salt. Add the mushrooms, chilli rings, and garlic, and simmer over medium heat, 3 minutes.

2 Add the prawns and 15 ml (1 tbsp) lemon juice to the pan. Bring back to a boil and simmer just until the prawns turn pink, 1–2 minutes.

3 Add the coriander leaves and simmer, about 1 minute longer. Taste, and add more lemon juice or salt if needed.

ANNE SAYS
"The lime leaves and pieces of lemon grass are inedible, so remove them before serving, if you prefer."

¶◉¶ TO SERVE
Ladle the soup into warmed individual bowls. Serve immediately, garnished with the reserved coriander sprigs, if you like.

VARIATION

HOT AND SOUR FISH SOUP

In this Japanese soup, the heat comes from fresh root ginger, the sour element is provided by rice vinegar, and soy sauce takes the place of Thai fish sauce. Cubes of white fish and the Japanese seaweed nori *give this soup a wonderful flavour of the sea.*

1 Omit the prawns, mushrooms, lemon grass, chillies, garlic, lime leaves, and fish sauce. With a small knife, peel the skin from a 5 cm (2 inch) piece of fresh root ginger. With a chef's knife, slice the ginger thinly, cutting across the fibrous grain. Crush each slice with the flat of a knife. Set aside half of the slices. Stack the remaining slices; cut into fine strips.

Fresh coriander adds characteristic anise flavour to Thai hot and sour soup

Lime leaves and lemon grass contribute the sour element, with chilli for heat

2 Trim 4 spring onions and cut them across into 5 cm (2 inch) pieces, including the green tops. Slice the pieces lengthwise into very fine strips. Strip the leaves from 4 sprigs of fresh coriander. Coarsely chop the leaves and reserve for garnish. Crush the stalks with the flat of the chef's knife.
3 Pour 1.5 litres (2⅓ pints) fish stock into a pan; add the ginger, coriander stalks, 60 ml (4 tbsp) rice vinegar, and 30 ml (2 tbsp) light soy sauce. Bring to a boil. Simmer, 15 minutes.
4 Meanwhile, rinse 375 g (12 oz) skinned plaice fillets and dry with paper towels. Cut into 2 cm (¾ inch) strips, then cut across into cubes.

5 Cut 1–2 sheets of dried Japanese seaweed (nori) into 2.5 cm (1 inch) squares; cut each one into 2 triangles.
6 Strain the stock into a saucepan. Stir in the ginger and spring onion strips, the fish, salt, and pepper. Bring just to a boil, and simmer until the fish just loses its transparency, 1–2 minutes.
7 Stir in the seaweed and simmer, 1 minute. Taste for seasoning. Serve, garnished with the chopped coriander.

CHICKEN CONSOMME WITH MADEIRA AND TOMATO

🍽 SERVES 4–6 　🥄 WORK TIME 50–60 MINUTES 　🍲 COOKING TIME 50–60 MINUTES

EQUIPMENT

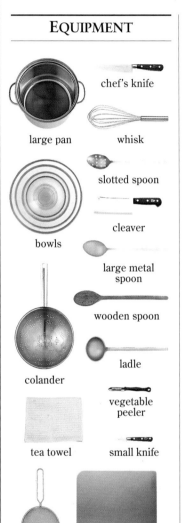

chef's knife

large pan　　whisk

slotted spoon

cleaver

bowls

large metal spoon

wooden spoon

ladle

colander

vegetable peeler

tea towel　　small knife

large sieve

baking sheet

paper towels　　chopping board

saucepans

serrated knife

INGREDIENTS

chicken wings and backs

tomatoes

egg whites

leeks

white bread

Madeira †

chicken stock

carrots

celery

† sherry can also be used

The flavour of homemade chicken consommé is incomparable. It should be based on concentrated homemade stock, clarified by whisking in egg whites which cook to form a filter. Aromatic vegetables and chicken bones are mixed with the egg whites for flavour. Madeira provides a rich note, and fine strips of tomato are the garnish.

GETTING AHEAD

The consommé and Melba toast can be made up to 3 days ahead; keep the consommé, covered, in the refrigerator and the Melba toast in an airtight container. Reheat the consommé and add the Madeira and tomato garnish just before serving.

metric	SHOPPING LIST	imperial
1.5 litres	chilled chicken stock (see box, page 125)	2⅓ pints
2	carrots	2
2	celery sticks	2
2	leeks, green part only	2
750 g	medium tomatoes	1½ lb
375 g	chicken wings and backs	12 oz
3	egg whites	3
	salt and pepper	
60 ml	Madeira, more if needed	2 fl oz
	For the Melba toast	
6	medium slices of white bread	6

ORDER OF WORK

1　PREPARE THE INGREDIENTS FOR CLARIFYING

2　CLARIFY THE CONSOMME

3　MAKE THE MELBA TOAST AND TOMATO GARNISH

4　FINISH THE CONSOMME

1 PREPARE THE INGREDIENTS FOR CLARIFYING

1 Using the large metal spoon, skim off any fat from the surface of the chilled chicken stock.

2 Gently heat the stock in the large pan until very warm. Draw a paper towel across the surface to remove any fat. Let cool. Meanwhile, prepare the vegetables and chicken.

ANNE SAYS
"Here I give instructions for preparing the vegetables by hand or machine. The choice is yours."

3 Peel the carrots; trim off the ends. Cut each carrot into 7.5 cm (3 inch) pieces. Cut each piece lengthwise into quarters to make sticks. Gather the sticks and cut across into medium dice.

ANNE SAYS
"Cut carrots into medium dice so they hold together during cooking and do not cloud the consommé."

To make dicing easy, cut carrot into sticks first

4 Cut the celery stalks into 7.5 cm (3 inch) pieces, then cut each piece lengthwise in half. Stack the halves and cut across into medium dice.

5 Slit the leeks lengthwise in half, then slit into quarters. Cut them crosswise into 5 mm (1/4 inch) slices. Wash the chopped leeks thoroughly in a bowl of cold water, then lift them out and drain in the colander.

HOW TO CHOP VEGETABLES IN A FOOD PROCESSOR

To save time, you can chop the vegetables for the consommé in a food processor.

Peel and trim the carrots and cut them into chunks. Cut the celery into chunks. Slit the leeks, cut them crosswise into 2–3 pieces, and wash them thoroughly. Combine all the vegetables in a food processor and work until roughly chopped. Peel and seed the tomatoes and cut each half into 2–3 pieces. Add to the vegetables and continue working until the tomatoes are chopped.

Tomatoes are strained from soup so they need not be peeled

6 Cut three-quarters of the tomatoes crosswise in half and squeeze out the seeds. Coarsely chop each half. Reserve the remaining tomatoes for garnish.

Seeds pop out when tomato half is squeezed

7 Using the small knife, remove and discard the skin and any fat from the chicken wings and backs. Rinse them and dry on paper towels.

Weight of cleaver splits chicken backs easily

Chicken bones are cut into small pieces so maximum flavour is extracted

8 Using the cleaver, carefully chop the chicken wings and backs into small even pieces.

2 CLARIFY THE CONSOMME

1 In a large bowl, whisk the egg whites until they are frothy. Add the vegetables, chicken pieces, salt, and pepper and stir with a spoon until well mixed.

Mix well so whisked egg whites are dispersed throughout vegetables and chicken

Tomatoes help give consommé good colour

2 Pour the cooled stock into the vegetable, chicken, and egg white mixture and stir together well.

! TAKE CARE !
The egg whites, vegetables, and chicken must be thoroughly mixed with the stock before heating or they will separate.

3 Return the mixture to the pan and bring slowly to a boil, whisking constantly, about 10 minutes. As soon as the liquid is frothy and starts to look white, stop whisking. When the stock simmers, the egg whites and the flavourings will form a layer on the surface. This layer is known as the clarification filter.

4 Lower the heat and, with the ladle, make a hole in the clarification filter or "raft" so the consommé can bubble away without breaking up the filter completely.

5 Simmer the consommé until it is clear and the clarification filter has formed a solid crust, 30–40 minutes. Meanwhile, make the Melba toast and tomato garnish (see page 26).

6 Set the sieve over a clean saucepan. Dampen the tea towel and use it to line the sieve. Taste the consommé and add salt and pepper if needed. Ladle the consommé into the lined sieve, breaking the clarification filter into pieces. Let the consommé drain slowly through the sieve into the saucepan.

! TAKE CARE !
Do not press on the solids of the clarification filter because this would make the consommé cloudy.

Vegetables and chicken yield their flavour during long cooking and are discarded with filter

Filter breaks in pieces when consommé is strained

7 Quickly draw a paper towel across the surface of the consommé to remove any remaining fat.

3 MAKE THE MELBA TOAST AND TOMATO GARNISH

Lightly toasted bread is cut into neat triangles

Steady serrated knife with your knuckles

1 Heat the oven to 170°C (325°F, Gas 3). Toast the bread on the baking sheet until light brown, 7–9 minutes. Cut off the crusts.

2 Place your palm on each slice and split the bread horizontally, cutting between the toasted surfaces. Cut the wafer-thin slices into triangles.

3 Lay the triangles, toasted-side down, on the baking sheet. Bake until crisp and curled, about 10 minutes.

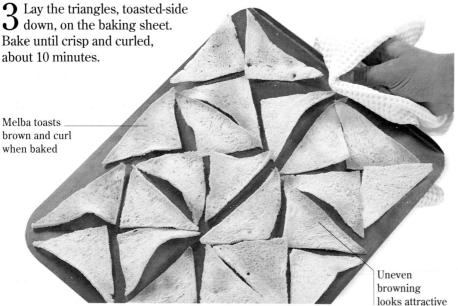

Melba toasts brown and curl when baked

Uneven browning looks attractive

4 Cut the cores from the reserved tomatoes and score an "x" on the base of each. Immerse them in boiling water until the skins start to split, 8–15 seconds depending on ripeness. Using the slotted spoon, transfer the tomatoes at once to a bowl of cold water. When cool, peel off the skins.

5 With the small knife, cut away sections of the fleshy outside of the tomato, leaving the interior and seeds. Place the pieces of tomato, cut-side up, on the chopping board and slice into very thin strips.

Slice in a curve to remove maximum of flesh

Interior of tomato and seeds are left behind

4 FINISH THE CONSOMME

Add Madeira to hot consommé just before serving so it does not evaporate

1 Bring the consommé almost to a boil, then stir in the Madeira. Taste, and add more if needed.

Fine slivers of tomato garnish show through golden consommé

VARIATION

CHICKEN CONSOMME WITH ORANGE

Orange gives a refreshing tang to this chicken consommé, which is garnished with a julienne of orange zest.

1 Omit the tomato garnish. Prepare the ingredients for clarifying as directed. Grate the zest from 2 oranges, using the coarsest grid of the grater.
2 Add the orange zest to the egg white mixture and clarify the consommé as directed.
3 Using a vegetable peeler, pare strips of zest from 1 large orange. Using a chef's knife, cut the pared orange zest into very fine julienne strips. Bring a small pan of water to a boil, add the orange julienne, simmer, 2 minutes, then drain. Rinse with cold water and drain again.
4 Reheat the consommé and stir in the Madeira.
5 Divide the orange julienne between warmed soup bowls and ladle the hot consommé on top of it. Serve with Melba toast, if you like.

¶◎¶ TO SERVE
Divide the tomato strips evenly between 4–6 soup cups and ladle the hot consommé over them. Serve the Melba toast separately.

Good consommé is crystal clear, with Melba toast as the classic accompaniment

CHINESE GREENS AND WONTON SOUP

🍽 SERVES 8   🥣 WORK TIME 1–1¼ HOURS   🍲 COOKING TIME 20–25 MINUTES

EQUIPMENT

chef's knife

palette knife

large pan

slotted spoon

wooden spoon

ladle

small
frying pan

small knife

ovenproof
dish

tray

colander   bowls

aluminium foil

sieve

tea towels

chopping board

*Broccoli and gai choy strike
a colourful note in this Chinese
soup. The wontons enclose a succulent filling of
pork, water chestnuts, cloud ears, and ginger.*

GETTING AHEAD

The wontons can be filled and the vegetables prepared up to
8 hours ahead; keep them, covered, in the refrigerator. Cook
the wontons and finish the soup just before serving.

metric	SHOPPING LIST	imperial
1	small head of broccoli, weighing about 250 g (8 oz)	1
250 g	gai choy (Chinese mustard greens)	8 oz
2 litres	chicken stock (see box, page 125)	3¼ pints
25 ml	soy sauce, more if needed	1½ tbsp
30 ml	rice wine, more if needed	2 tbsp
10 ml	sesame oil, more if needed	2 tsp
	salt and pepper	
	For the wontons	
7 g	dried Chinese cloud ears or dried mushrooms	¼ oz
4	canned water chestnuts, total weight about 30 g (1 oz)	4
4	spring onions	4
2.5 cm	piece of fresh root ginger	1 inch
1	garlic clove	1
175 g	lean minced pork	6 oz
5 ml	cornflour	1 tsp
1	large pinch of crushed chillies	1
15 ml	soy sauce	1 tbsp
15 ml	rice wine	1 tbsp
32	wonton wrappers, total weight about 125 g (4 oz)	32

INGREDIENTS

wonton
wrappers

soy
sauce

gai choy †

water
chestnuts

minced
pork

sesame
oil

dried Chinese
cloud ears

garlic
clove

rice
wine ‡

fresh
root ginger

chicken
stock

cornflour

crushed
chillies

broccoli

spring onions

† bok choy or Chinese leaves can
also be used
‡ dry sherry can also be used

ORDER OF WORK

**1 PREPARE THE
FILLING AND FILL
THE WONTONS**

**2 PREPARE THE
VEGETABLES**

3 MAKE THE SOUP

1 PREPARE THE FILLING AND FILL THE WONTONS

1 Put the dried cloud ears into a bowl, cover with hot water, and set aside to soften, about 15 minutes.

2 Pat the water chestnuts dry. Slice them, then finely chop them with the chef's knife.

Green tops of spring onions add colour and mild flavour to filling

3 Trim the spring onions and cut them across into 7.5 cm (3 inch) pieces, including the green tops. Slice them lengthwise into very fine strips, then cut across the strips to make dice.

4 Peel the root ginger. Using the chef's knife, slice it thinly, cutting across the grain. Crush each slice with the flat of the chef's knife and chop finely. Lightly crush the garlic clove with the flat of the knife. Discard the skin and finely chop the garlic.

5 Drain the cloud ears and squeeze them in your fist to remove excess water. Cut off any stalks. Cut each cloud ear into fine strips, then cut across the strips to make dice.

6 Put the cloud ears, water chestnuts, spring onions, root ginger, and garlic into a bowl. Add the pork, cornflour, crushed chillies, soy sauce, rice wine, salt, and pepper and mix well with the wooden spoon.

Chinese cloud ear fungus combines delicate flavour with crunchy texture

7 Shape a small ball of filling. Heat the small frying pan, add the ball of filling, and fry until brown on both sides. Taste it, and add more seasoning to the remaining filling if necessary.

8 Place a wonton wrapper flat on the work surface. Put 5 ml (1 tsp) of the filling in the centre. With your finger, moisten 2 adjacent sides, then fold the dry sides over the dampened ones to form a triangle. Press the sides together to seal them.

ANNE SAYS
"While you work, keep the remaining wonton wrappers covered with a damp tea towel or plastic wrap so that they do not dry out."

Filling goes right in centre of wonton wrapper

9 Roll the filling gently towards the point of the triangle, plumping up the filling and making a crease.

10 Moisten the left corner of the triangle. Pull towards the centre, in front of the filling, and bring the right corner in to cover the left. Press the 2 corners together to seal them and to plump up the filling.

11 Set the shaped wonton on a tray and cover with a damp tea towel. Continue filling and shaping the wontons, keeping them covered as soon as they are completed.

2 PREPARE THE VEGETABLES

1 With the small knife, cut off the broccoli heads, discarding the stalks. Cut the heads into florets.

2 Using the chef's knife, trim the ends of the stalks of the gai choy. Wash all the greens thoroughly in cold water and drain them well. Cut the stems from the gai choy leaves. Gather the stalks together into a pile and cut across into thin slices.

3 Stack the gai choy leaves and roll them loosely, then cut across into fine shreds with the chef's knife.

ANNE SAYS
"If using bok choy, cut it lengthwise in half, then slice across into shreds."

3 MAKE THE SOUP

1 Bring the stock to a boil in the large pan. Stir in the soy sauce and rice wine. Add about half of the wontons in a single layer. Simmer, turning them carefully, until they are tender and translucent, 5–7 minutes. To test, lift out one of the wontons and taste it.

Wontons are carefully lowered into hot stock

2 With the slotted spoon, lift out the cooked wontons and place them, side by side, in the ovenproof dish. Ladle a little stock over them to keep them moist. Cover and keep warm while you cook the remaining wontons.

3 Add the gai choy and broccoli to the pan. Return to a boil and simmer, 1–2 minutes. Remove from the heat and stir in the sesame oil. Taste the soup and add more oil, soy sauce, rice wine, salt, and pepper if needed.

🍽 TO SERVE

Divide the wontons among 8 warmed bowls and ladle the soup over them. If you like, serve extra sesame oil and soy sauce in small bowls for guests to help themselves.

Shredded gai choy and broccoli
add colour to soup

VARIATION

MUSHROOM WONTON SOUP

Here, wonton soup takes on a European flavour.

1 Omit the broccoli, gai choy, soy sauce, rice wine, sesame oil, and pork filling mixture.

2 Soak 30 g (1 oz) dried boletus mushrooms in 125 ml (4 fl oz) warm water in a bowl, about 20 minutes. Wipe the caps of 250 g (8 oz) button mushrooms, trim the stalks, then dice.

3 Finely chop 1 garlic clove. Peel 2 shallots, leaving a little root. Slice horizontally then vertically towards the root, leaving the slices attached. Dice.

4 Strip the leaves from 4–6 sprigs of flat-leaf parsley. Reserve 8 leaves. Finely chop the remaining leaves.

5 Drain the dried mushrooms; reserve the soaking liquid. Slice, then finely chop.

6 Heat 30 g (1 oz) butter in a frying pan, add all of the mushrooms, the garlic, shallots, salt, and pepper. Cook over high heat, stirring occasionally, 10–15 minutes. Stir in the chopped parsley; taste for seasoning. Let cool.

7 Fill the wontons with the cooled mushroom mixture and shape as directed. Cut 125 g (4 oz) thinly sliced Parma ham into thin strips. Bring the stock to a boil and add 45 ml (3 tbsp) Madeira and the reserved mushroom soaking liquid. Cook the wontons as directed.

8 Divide the wontons among warmed bowls. Ladle in the soup and finish with the Parma ham and parsley. Serve hot.

MUSHROOM AND WILD RICE SOUP

🍴 SERVES 4–6 🥄 WORK TIME 35–40 MINUTES 🍲 COOKING TIME 45–50 MINUTES

EQUIPMENT

chef's knife

small ladle†

bowls

ladle

rolling pin

bowl sieve

vegetable peeler

conical sieve

paper towels

saucepans, 1 with lid

chopping board

†wooden spoon can also be used

INGREDIENTS

dried wild mushrooms

button mushrooms

garlic clove

fresh thyme

juniper berries

wild rice

port

butter

onion

bay leaf

celery stick

chicken stock

carrot

*Dried wild mushrooms are a favourite of mine –
you can use almost any type for this earthy soup.
Morels, boletus (ceps), shiitake, and Chinese
black mushrooms are especially good. Wild rice,
with its nutty taste, is the perfect finishing touch.*

GETTING AHEAD
The soup can be made up to 2 days ahead and kept,
covered, in the refrigerator. Reheat it and add the reserved
port wine just before serving.

metric	SHOPPING LIST	imperial
30 g	dried wild mushrooms	1 oz
375 ml	warm water	12 fl oz
250 g	button mushrooms	8 oz
1	onion	1
1	garlic clove	1
1	celery stick	1
1	carrot	1
6	sprigs of fresh thyme	6
4–6	juniper berries	4–6
60 g	butter	2 oz
125 ml	port	4 fl oz
1	bay leaf	1
1 litre	chicken stock (see box, page 125)	1²/₃ pints
100 g	wild rice	3¹/₂ oz
	salt and pepper	

ORDER OF WORK

1 PREPARE THE INGREDIENTS

2 MAKE THE MUSHROOM BROTH; PARBOIL THE WILD RICE AND FINISH SOUP

1 PREPARE THE INGREDIENTS

1 Put the dried mushrooms into a bowl, cover with the warm water, and soak until soft, about 30 minutes.

2 Meanwhile, wipe the button mushroom caps with damp paper towels and trim the stalks even with the caps. Set the mushrooms stalk-side down and evenly slice them. Reserve 45 g (1½ oz) of the mushroom slices. Roughly chop the remainder.

3 Peel the onion, leaving a little of the root attached, and cut it lengthwise in half. Slice each half horizontally towards the root, leaving the slices attached at the root end, then slice vertically, again leaving the root end uncut. Cut across to make dice.

4 Set the flat side of the chef's knife on top of the garlic clove and strike it with your fist. Discard the skin.

5 Peel the strings from the celery with the vegetable peeler, reserving the leaves for decoration. Cut the stick across into 7.5 cm (3 inch) pieces, then cut each piece lengthwise into 2–3 strips. Stack the strips and cut across into dice.

6 Peel and trim the carrot. Cut it across into 5 cm (2 inch) pieces. Cut each piece lengthwise into 5 mm (¼ inch) slices. Stack the slices and cut each stack into 4–6 strips. Gather the strips together into a pile and cut them crosswise into dice.

Vegetables are cut into quite small dice so all their flavour is extracted during simmering

Carrots add natural sweetness to vegetable broth

7 Strip the leaves from half of the thyme sprigs with your fingertips and set the leaves aside.

8 Put the juniper berries into a small bowl and crush with the end of the rolling pin.

Juniper berries have piquant spiciness

Liquid from soaking mushrooms is reserved for soup

9 Drain the dried mushrooms, reserving the liquid. Rinse the mushrooms under cold water and drain them on paper towels.

ANNE SAYS
"Dried wild mushrooms are usually sold sliced. If using whole mushrooms, slice them after soaking."

Paper towels soak up excess liquid

10 Line the bowl sieve with a paper towel and set it over a bowl. Pour the mushroom soaking liquid into the sieve; the paper towel will remove any grit.

2 MAKE THE MUSHROOM BROTH; PARBOIL THE WILD RICE AND FINISH SOUP

2 Stir in the chopped button mushrooms, mushroom soaking liquid, half of the port, the juniper berries, thyme sprigs, bay leaf, chicken stock, salt, and pepper. Bring to a boil, then cover the pan, and simmer, 30 minutes. Meanwhile, parboil the wild rice.

Juniper berries and port add richness to soup

Mushrooms and vegetables are simmered in stock for maximum flavour

1 Melt the butter in a large saucepan, add the onion, garlic, carrot, and celery and sauté, stirring occasionally, until golden brown, 5–7 minutes.

3 Bring a medium pan of salted water to a boil, add the wild rice, and bring back to a boil. Cover, and simmer until the rice is almost tender, 30 minutes. Drain the rice.

4 Strain the vegetable broth through the conical sieve into another large saucepan, pressing on the vegetables and herbs with the small ladle to extract all their flavour.

5 Bring the strained vegetable broth to a boil. Add the reserved sliced button mushrooms, the soaked dried mushrooms, reserved thyme leaves, and parboiled wild rice. Simmer until the rice is tender, 15–20 minutes. Stir in the remaining port and taste the soup for seasoning.

¶◎¶ TO SERVE

Ladle into warmed individual soup plates, decorate with the reserved celery leaves, and serve immediately.

Wild mushrooms add unique earthy flavour to soup

Wild rice adds body as well as nutty taste

VARIATION

CREAM OF MUSHROOM AND RICE SOUP

Here the subtle flavour of button mushrooms is highlighted with cream, and the soup is thickened with white rice.

1 Omit the dried wild mushrooms, juniper berries, port, and wild rice.
2 Use 500 g (1 lb) button mushrooms and chop them all as directed. Prepare the onion, garlic, carrot, and celery as directed. Strip all the thyme leaves from the sprigs.
3 Make the broth as directed, adding the thyme leaves with the bay leaf. Do not strain the broth.
4 While the broth is simmering, cook 100 g (3½ oz) long-grain rice in boiling salted water until tender, 10–12 minutes. Drain and set aside.
5 Remove and discard the bay leaf from the broth, then purée the broth in a blender until finely chopped but not smooth, working in several batches if necessary.
6 Return the mushroom soup to the pan and stir in the rice and 250 ml (8 fl oz) single cream.
7 Heat the soup until very hot, but do not boil or it may curdle. Remove from the heat, stir in 30 ml (2 tbsp) chopped chives, taste for seasoning, and ladle into warmed soup plates. Decorate with 2 crossed whole chives.

SPICED CARROT AND ORANGE SOUP

 SERVES 6 WORK TIME 30–35 MINUTES COOKING TIME 30–40 MINUTES

EQUIPMENT

grater

hand blender †

chef's knife

ladle

sieve

wooden spoon

vegetable peeler

lemon squeezer

saucepans, 1 with lid

chopping board

INGREDIENTS

carrots

single cream

oranges

ground coriander

onion

butter

chicken stock

The carrots in our Burgundy garden are renowned – they are huge and craggy with an astonishing sweetness of flavour. Given their enormous size, soup is an obvious destiny, and I'm particularly fond of this recipe, which is flavoured with orange and a warm spicing of ground coriander. A bold zigzag of cream and a sprinkling of orange julienne make a stylish presentation.

GETTING AHEAD
The soup and the orange julienne can be made up to 2 days ahead and kept, covered, in the refrigerator. Reheat the soup and add the cream and orange julienne just before serving.

metric	SHOPPING LIST	imperial
750 g	carrots	1½ lb
1	onion	1
2	oranges	2
30 g	butter	1 oz
7.5 ml	ground coriander, more if needed	1½ tsp
	salt and pepper	
1 litre	chicken stock (see page 125), more if needed	1⅔ pints
175 ml	single cream	6 fl oz

ORDER OF WORK

1 PREPARE AND MAKE THE SOUP

2 FINISH THE SOUP

† standard blender or food processor can also be used

1 PREPARE AND MAKE THE SOUP

1 Peel the carrots and trim off the ends. With the chef's knife, cut each carrot into thin slices.

Large carrots are ideal for soup

Slice carrots evenly so they cook at same speed

2 Peel the onion, leaving a little of the root attached, and cut it in half through the root and stalk. Lay each onion half flat on the chopping board and slice horizontally towards the root, leaving the slices attached at the root end, then slice vertically, again leaving the root end uncut. Finally, cut across the onion to make dice.

3 Grate the zest from 1 orange. Make julienne strips from the zest of the other orange (see box, page 38). Squeeze the juice from both oranges; measure 125 ml (4 fl oz) juice.

Grated zest is cooked with vegetables

Orange juice brings out natural sweetness of carrots

4 Melt the butter in a large saucepan and add the onion. Cook, stirring until soft but not brown, 2–3 minutes.

5 Add the carrots, grated orange zest, ground coriander, salt, and pepper and stir to mix together with the onion. Cover the saucepan and cook gently, stirring occasionally, about 10 minutes.

ANNE SAYS
"This slow cooking mellows the flavour of the orange zest and coriander."

Ground coriander adds warmth to flavour of orange

6 Add the chicken stock and bring to a boil. Lower the heat, cover the pan again, and simmer, stirring occasionally, until the vegetables are very tender, 30–40 minutes.

ANNE SAYS
"Here the chicken stock develops the flavour of sautéed carrots and onions, and mellows the orange zest and coriander."

Carrots simmer gently in chicken stock

Vegetables will soften when simmered in stock

Using a hand blender, soup can be puréed in cooking pan

7 Let the soup cool slightly, then purée it in the saucepan with the hand blender; or purée the soup in a food processor or a standard blender, in 2–3 batches if necessary.

HOW TO MAKE ORANGE JULIENNE

Thin strips of orange zest make an attractive garnish for sweet and savoury dishes flavoured with orange juice. They are usually blanched in boiling water to remove bitterness.

Pare zest carefully to avoid bitter-tasting pith

1 Using a vegetable peeler, pare the zest from the orange, leaving behind the white pith.

2 With a chef's knife, cut the pared strips of orange zest into the thinnest possible julienne strips.

3 Drop the strips in boiling water and simmer, 2 minutes. Drain. Rinse with cold water. Drain again.

2 FINISH THE SOUP

1 Reheat the carrot soup, then stir in the orange juice and 125 ml (4 fl oz) of the cream. If the soup is too thick, stir in more stock. Taste the soup for seasoning, adding more coriander, salt, and pepper if needed.

ANNE SAYS
"Do not continue to cook the soup or the orange juice will become bitter."

2 Ladle the soup into warmed individual soup plates. With the remaining cream, make a bold zigzag on the surface of each serving, using a teaspoon.

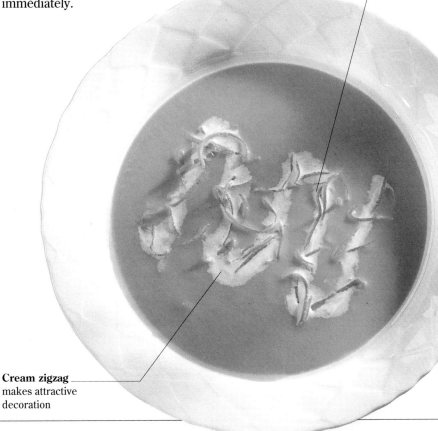

Cream is easy to control when poured from spoon

🍴 TO SERVE

Sprinkle each serving with some of the orange julienne and serve immediately.

Orange julienne gives a hint of flavouring in the soup

Cream zigzag makes attractive decoration

VARIATION

SPICED CARROT AND PARSNIP SOUP

Cumin is the subtle spicing here, with fine strips of carrot and parsnip as the garnish.

1 Omit the oranges. Peel and chop the onion as directed.
2 Use 500 g (1 lb) carrots and 250 g (8 oz) parsnips. Reserve 1/2 carrot and 1/2 parsnip to make the julienne for the garnish; peel and thinly slice the remaining carrots and parsnips.
3 Make the soup as directed, using ground cumin instead of coriander.
4 Meanwhile, prepare the julienne garnish: peel the reserved carrot and parsnip halves and trim off the ends. Set the halves cut-side down and cut into very thin slices. Stack the slices and cut lengthwise into fine strips.
5 Pour enough vegetable oil into a small saucepan to come one-third of the way up the side, and heat until hot enough to brown a cube of fresh bread in 40 seconds. If using a deep-fat thermometer, it should register 190°C (375°F). Add the vegetable strips and deep-fry, stirring until golden brown, 30–60 seconds. Lift the vegetables out with a slotted spoon and drain on paper towels.
6 Spoon the hot soup into warmed bowls, sprinkle with the carrot and parsnip strips, and serve at once.

PEPPERY GREEN SOUP

🍴 SERVES 6   🥄 WORK TIME 25–35 MINUTES   🍲 COOKING TIME ABOUT 10 MINUTES

EQUIPMENT

chef's knife

whisk

blender†

ladle

rubber spatula

small knife

large pan

frying pan

colander

baking sheet

large saucepan

chopping board

† food processor can also be used

Spinach, rocket, and watercress are cooked briefly to keep their fresh colour, then puréed until finely chopped but not completely smooth. The resulting soup is a rich green, with a contrasting garnish of cream and toasted almonds. If rocket is not available, use more watercress.

GETTING AHEAD

The soup can be made up to 2 days ahead; keep it, covered, in the refrigerator. Just before serving, reheat the soup, stir in the cream and lemon juice, and add the cream decoration and toasted almond garnish.

metric	SHOPPING LIST	imperial
375 g	spinach	12 oz
125 g	watercress	4 oz
125 g	rocket	4 oz
	salt and pepper	
60 g	flaked almonds	2 oz
2	shallots	2
45 g	butter	1½ oz
30 g	plain flour	1 oz
1.5 litres	chicken stock (see box, page 125)	2⅓ pints
1	pinch of ground nutmeg, more if needed	1
125 ml	double cream, plus 60 ml (4 tbsp) for decoration	4 fl oz
	juice of 1 lemon	

INGREDIENTS

spinach

watercress

shallots

rocket

plain flour

butter

chicken stock

flaked almonds

ground nutmeg

lemon juice

double cream

ORDER OF WORK

1 PREPARE THE GREENS

2 PREPARE THE GARNISH AND MAKE THE SOUP

40

1 PREPARE THE GREENS

Small tender spinach leaves are used for soup

1 Discard the ribs and stalks from the spinach, watercress, and rocket. Wash the leaves thoroughly in plenty of cold water.

2 Fill the large pan with salted water, bring to a boil, and add the greens, pushing them down under the water. Simmer until tender, 1–2 minutes. Drain the greens in the colander. Rinse immediately under cold running water to set their bright colour and drain again thoroughly.

Greens will purée easily if you add a little chicken stock

3 When the greens are cool enough to handle, squeeze them to remove excess water. Put them in the blender and purée until finely chopped, scraping the container with the rubber spatula. Alternatively, purée the greens in a food processor.

HOW TO CHOP A SHALLOT

For a standard chop, make slices that are about 3 mm (1/8 inch) thick. For a fine chop, slice the shallot as thinly as possible.

1 Peel the outer papery skin from the shallot. (If necessary, separate the shallot into sections at the root and peel the sections.) Cut rounded shallots in half. Set each shallot, flat-side down, on a chopping board and slice it horizontally, leaving the slices attached at the root end.

2 Holding it steady, slice vertically through the shallot, again leaving the root end uncut.

3 Cut across the shallot to make fine dice. Continue chopping, if necessary, until it is very fine.

2 PREPARE THE GARNISH AND MAKE THE SOUP

1 Heat the oven to 180°C (350°F, Gas 4). Spread the almonds on the baking sheet and toast until lightly browned, 6–8 minutes. Stir occasionally so they colour evenly. Let cool.

Toast almonds carefully since they scorch easily

2 Chop the shallots (see box, page 41). Melt the butter in the saucepan, add the shallots, and sauté until soft but not brown, 2–3 minutes. Whisk in the flour and cook, stirring constantly, until foaming and straw-coloured, 1–2 minutes.

CREAM DECORATIONS FOR SOUPS

Patterns made with double cream are an attractive finishing touch for puréed soups. These three designs make simple but very effective decorations.

CIRCLE OF HEARTS	FLOWER	PINWHEEL

CIRCLE OF HEARTS

1 From the tip of a teaspoon, drip cream onto the surface of the soup to form a circle of drops.

2 Draw the tip of a small knife through the drops to create a circle of hearts.

FLOWER

1 Using a teaspoon, drizzle a circle of cream onto the surface of each plate of soup.

2 Feather by drawing the tip of a knife crosswise through the cream, first in one direction, then the other.

PINWHEEL

1 Place about 15 ml (1 tbsp) of cream on the surface of each plate of soup.

2 Draw the tip of a small knife away from the centre to make an even pattern of curved spokes.

3 Whisk in the stock and bring to a boil, stirring until the soup boils and thickens. Add the nutmeg, salt, and pepper and simmer, 2 minutes.

4 Add the puréed greens to the soup and bring almost back to a boil, whisking vigorously.

5 Whisk in the 125 ml (4 fl oz) cream, bring just back to a boil, and remove from the heat. Add 30 ml (2 tbsp) lemon juice and taste, adding more lemon juice, salt, and pepper if needed.

ANNE SAYS
"Stir in the lemon juice just before serving otherwise the soup may lose its brilliant colour."

🍽 TO SERVE
Ladle the soup into 6 warmed soup plates and make a flower or other decoration on each serving with the remaining cream (see box, page 42). Sprinkle with a few toasted almonds, and pass the rest around separately.

V A R I A T I O N
PEPPERY GREEN SOUP WITH CHORIZO
Slices of spicy chorizo sausage are added here, and the soup is given a little kick of Tabasco.

1 Omit the double cream and toasted almonds. Prepare the spinach, watercress, rocket, and shallots and make the soup as directed.
2 Cut 250 g (8 oz) chorizo or other spicy sausage crosswise into very thin slices. Heat 15 ml (1 tbsp) vegetable oil in a frying pan, add the sausage slices and sauté until almost crisp and much of the sausage fat has been rendered, 5–7 minutes. Drain the sausage slices on paper towels.
3 Reheat the soup if necessary. Stir in 2–3 dashes of Tabasco sauce and add the sausage slices. Serve hot.

Cream mellows the peppery taste of rocket and watercress

Toasted almonds add crunchy texture to this smooth soup

CHEDDAR AND VEGETABLE SOUP

 SERVES 10 WORK TIME 40–45 MINUTES COOKING TIME 30–35 MINUTES

EQUIPMENT

chef's knife

slotted spoon

food processor†

vegetable peeler

wooden spoon

ladle

paper towels

medium frying pan

grater

large pan, with lid

chopping board

†blender can also be used

Carrots and sweet potatoes give this cream of vegetable soup smoothness and brilliant colour. Mature Cheddar cheese provides richness, with the flavour accented by Worcestershire sauce. For serving, each bowl is topped with crisp bacon, diced cheese, and chopped parsley, making it hearty enough for a main course.

GETTING AHEAD
The soup can be made up to 2 days ahead and kept, covered, in the refrigerator. Just before serving, reheat the soup, then stir in the cheese, and add the garnish.

metric	SHOPPING LIST	imperial
2	onions	2
375 g	carrots	12 oz
375 g	sweet potatoes	12 oz
2	celery sticks	2
375 g	baking potatoes	12 oz
1.5 litres	chicken stock (see box, page 125)	2⅓ pints
	salt and pepper	
175 g	bacon rashers	6 oz
5–7	sprigs of parsley	5–7
175 g	mature Cheddar cheese	6 oz
500 ml	milk	16 fl oz
125 ml	double cream	4 fl oz
15 ml	Worcestershire sauce, more if needed	1 tbsp

INGREDIENTS

mature Cheddar cheese

bacon rashers

onions

carrots

baking potatoes   sweet potatoes

celery sticks

double cream

milk

parsley

chicken stock

Worcestershire sauce

ORDER OF WORK

1 PREPARE AND COOK THE VEGETABLES

2 PREPARE THE GARNISH

3 FINISH THE SOUP

1 PREPARE AND COOK THE VEGETABLES

1 Peel the onions, leaving a little of the root attached, and cut them lengthwise in half. Set each half cut-side down and slice horizontally, then vertically towards the root, leaving the slices attached. Cut into dice.

2 Peel the carrots and trim the ends. Cut each carrot into 7.5 cm (3 inch) pieces. Cut each piece lengthwise into quarters to make sticks. Gather the sticks into a pile and cut across into neat dice.

3 Using the vegetable peeler, peel the sweet potatoes. With the chef's knife, cut them lengthwise into 5 mm (¼ inch) slices. Stack the slices and cut into 5 mm (¼ inch) strips. Gather the strips into a pile and cut crosswise into dice.

Peel sweet potato lengthwise, holding it in one hand to ensure firm grip

Chicken stock adds flavour to vegetables

Vegetables cook at same speed when cut into even dice

4 Peel the strings from the celery with the vegetable peeler. Cut in half, then cut the halves lengthwise into strips. Cut the strips into dice. Peel the baking potatoes, then dice as for the sweet potatoes.

5 Put all the diced vegetables into the large pan, add the stock, salt, and pepper and bring to a boil. Cover and simmer until the vegetables are very tender, 25–30 minutes. Meanwhile, prepare the garnish.

2 PREPARE THE GARNISH

1 Stack the bacon rashers in a pile. Using the chef's knife, cut them crosswise into 5 mm (¼ inch) strips.

Bacon strips will shrink into crisp flakes when cooked

2 Put the bacon strips into the frying pan and fry, stirring, until browned and crisp, and the bacon fat is rendered, 3–5 minutes. Lift out with the slotted spoon and drain on paper towels.

Diced cheese is for garnish

Grated cheese will melt smoothly into hot soup

3 Strip the parsley leaves from the stalks with the tips of your fingers and pile them together on the chopping board. Using the chef's knife, finely chop the leaves.

4 Cut one-quarter of the cheese into 5 mm (¼ inch) slices. Cut the slices lengthwise into 5 mm (¼ inch) strips, then into dice; reserve for the garnish. Grate the remaining cheese.

3 FINISH THE SOUP

1 Ladle the cooked vegetables and liquid into the food processor and purée until smooth.

ANNE SAYS
"Puréeing may have to be done in two or more batches. Take care when handling if the soup is very hot."

2 Return the soup to the pan and stir in the milk, cream, and Worcestershire sauce, using the wooden spoon. Bring just to a boil, then lower the heat.

Double cream adds richness to soup

3 Gradually add the grated cheese, stirring over a low heat so it melts and blends evenly into the soup. Taste, and add more Worcestershire sauce, salt, and pepper if needed.

¶⊙¶ TO SERVE
Ladle the soup into a warmed tureen and garnish with the bacon, diced cheese, and chopped parsley.
Serve immediately.

Garnish makes lively colour contrast to cheese and vegetable soup

Crisp bacon strips add crunchy contrast to the smoothness of soup

V A R I A T I O N

BLUE CHEESE AND CELERIAC SOUP

White wine gives a little punch to this creamy soup. Roquefort, Danish Blue, and Stilton are all equally suitable blue cheeses. Serve with decoratively shaped toasted croûtes fringed with chopped parsley.

1 Omit the carrots, sweet potatoes, bacon, Cheddar cheese, and the Worcestershire sauce. Prepare the onions, celery sticks, and baking potatoes as directed.
2 Warm the chicken stock in a large saucepan. Peel 250 g (8 oz) celeriac and cut it into dice as for the baking potatoes. Drop the dice at once into the stock to prevent discoloration.

3 Add the onions, celery, baking potatoes, and 125 ml (4 fl oz) dry white wine to the stock, and cook as directed.
4 Chop 10 parsley sprigs as directed.

5 Crumble 125 g (4 oz) blue cheese.
6 Make toasted croûtes: heat the oven to 190°C (375°F, Gas 5). Using a pastry cutter, cut 10 decorative shapes from slices of white bread. Brush lightly on both sides with oil. Set the shapes on an ungreased baking sheet and toast, turning once, 5–12 minutes.
7 Dip the edges of the croûtes in half of the chopped parsley. Purée the soup as directed, and finish with the milk and cream. Reheat, then stir in three-quarters of the crumbled blue cheese. Taste for seasoning.
8 Ladle into warmed bowls. Garnish with the remaining blue cheese and parsley. Serve with the toasted croûtes.

ROASTED AUBERGINE SOUP WITH CHILLI CREAM

🍽 SERVES 6 　🥣 WORK TIME 55–60 MINUTES* 　🍲 COOKING TIME 15 MINUTES

EQUIPMENT

chef's knife

ladle

small knife

food processor †

paper towels

baking sheets

saucepans

rubber spatula

rubber gloves

chopping board

ANNE SAYS
"*Aubergines can vary considerably in size, so you may need more than one baking sheet to spread them out in a single layer.*"

†blender can also be used

Roasted aubergines, with their rich smokiness, form the base for this unusual soup. Sesame-seed twists are the suggested accompaniment.

— GETTING AHEAD —

The soup and chilli cream can be made up to 1 day ahead; keep them separately, covered, in the refrigerator. Just before serving, reheat the soup and add the warmed chilli cream

* plus 30 minutes standing time

metric	SHOPPING LIST	imperial
1.15 kg	aubergines	2¹/₂ lb
	salt and pepper	
	olive oil for baking sheets	
4	large shallots, weighing about 250 g (8 oz)	4
4	garlic cloves	4
1 litre	chicken stock (see box, page 125)	1²/₃ pints
	juice of ¹/₂ lemon, more if needed	
1.25 ml	ground cinnamon	¹/₄ tsp
	sesame-seed twists (see box, page 49) for serving (optional)	
	For the chilli cream	
1–2	fresh hot red chillies	1–2
1	small red pepper	1
125 ml	chicken stock	4 fl oz
90 ml	double cream	3 fl oz

INGREDIENTS

aubergines

fresh hot red chillies

lemon juice

olive oil

chicken stock

garlic cloves

ground cinnamon

red pepper

shallots

double cream

sesame-seed twists (optional)

ORDER OF WORK

1 **ROAST THE VEGETABLES**

2 **MAKE THE CHILLI CREAM**

3 **MAKE THE SOUP**

1 ROAST THE VEGETABLES

1 Put the aubergines on the chopping board. Using the chef's knife, trim and cut them lengthwise in half.

2 Score the flesh in a lattice, cutting almost to the skin. Set the aubergines, cut-side up, and sprinkle generously with salt. Let stand to draw out the bitter juices, 30 minutes.

SESAME-SEED TWISTS

These twists with their spicy, nutty taste make a good accompaniment for robust, strongly flavoured soups. They also make an attractive nibble to serve with drinks. Sesame-seed twists can be made the day before they are required and stored in an airtight container. Take care when you handle them because they are very fragile when baked.

 MAKES 24

⏲ **WORK TIME 8–10 MINUTES***

🍲 **COOKING TIME ABOUT 10 MINUTES**

* *plus at least 15 minutes chilling time*

SHOPPING LIST

	plain flour for dusting	
250 g	puff pastry dough	8 oz
1	egg	1
2.5 ml	salt	½ tsp
25 ml	sesame seeds	1½ tbsp

1 Sprinkle a baking sheet with water. On a lightly floured surface, roll out the puff pastry dough to a rectangle approximately 20 x 30 cm (8 x 12) inches. Trim edges with a chef's knife.

2 Lightly beat the egg with the salt. Brush the pastry dough with the egg glaze. Sprinkle the sesame seeds evenly over the dough and press them down lightly.

3 Cut the dough into twenty-four 1.25 cm (½ inch) strips. Lift each strip and twist it along its length several times, then lay it on the baking sheet, pressing each end firmly to secure it. Chill the twists until firm, at least 15 minutes. Meanwhile, heat the oven to 220°C (425°F, Gas 7).

4 Bake the twists in the heated oven until crisp and golden brown, about 10 minutes. Loosen the twists from the baking sheet, transfer to a wire rack, and let cool.

3 Heat the oven to 180°C (350°F, Gas 4). Lightly brush 1–2 baking sheets with olive oil. Rinse the cut surfaces of the aubergine halves with cold water to remove the salt.

4 Arrange the aubergine halves, cut-side down, in a single layer on the baking sheets. Roast in the heated oven, 10 minutes.

Root and top are left to hold shallot together

Press vegetables with your finger to test if they are tender

5 If necessary, separate the sections of the shallots. Pull off and discard any loose skin but do not peel the shallots.

6 Set the shallots on the baking sheets with the aubergines. Add the garlic cloves, in their skins. Continue roasting the vegetables until they are soft, 35–45 minutes longer. Meanwhile, make the chilli cream.

2 MAKE THE CHILLI CREAM

1 Core, seed, and dice the chillies (see box, page 51). Cut out the core of the red pepper and discard it. Halve the red pepper lengthwise and discard the seeds and white ribs.

Remove seeds and white ribs because they can be bitter

2 Set each red pepper half cut-side down, flatten it with the heel of your hand, and slice it lengthwise into thin strips. Gather the strips together and cut across to make neat dice.

HOW TO CORE, SEED, AND DICE FRESH HOT CHILLIES

Fresh hot chillies must be finely chopped so their heat is spread evenly through the dish. For a hotter flavour, you can add the seeds too. Chillies can burn your skin, so be sure to wear rubber gloves and avoid contact with your eyes.

Remove all seeds unless very hot flavour is wanted

1 Cut the chillies lengthwise in half with a small knife. Cut out the core and fleshy white ribs and scrape out the seeds.

2 Set each chilli half cut-side up and thinly slice it lengthwise into strips with the small knife.

3 Gather the chilli strips together with your fingers and cut them across to produce very fine dice.

3 Put the chilli, red pepper, and ½ cup chicken stock into a small saucepan. Bring to a boil and simmer until the peppers are very soft, about 10 minutes.

4 Drain the peppers and transfer them to the food processor or blender. Add the double cream, salt, and pepper, and purée until smooth. Taste the chilli cream for seasoning, then pour it into the small saucepan.

Chilli cream should have pouring consistency

3 MAKE THE SOUP

Roasted aubergine flesh can be scraped easily from skin

Flesh stays moist during baking as it is protected by skin

1 Remove the vegetables from the oven. When the aubergine halves are cool enough to handle, scoop out the flesh; put it into the food processor or blender. Discard the skins.

2 Cut the end off each shallot and garlic clove and squeeze the pulp into the food processor or blender. Purée the vegetables until smooth, occasionally scraping down the side of the bowl with the rubber spatula. If necessary, work them in 2 batches, adding a little of the chicken stock.

3 Transfer the vegetable purée to a large saucepan. Stir in the lemon juice, chicken stock, cinnamon, salt, and pepper. Bring to a boil and simmer, 10 minutes. Taste for seasoning, adding more lemon juice, salt, and pepper if needed.

🍽️ TO SERVE

Heat the chilli cream. Ladle the aubergine soup into warmed individual soup plates and swirl a little of the chilli cream in the centre of each one. Serve the remaining chilli cream separately, with sesame-seed twists, if you like.

ANNE SAYS
"The piquant chilli cream gives a lift to the smoky flavour of roasted aubergine."

Sesame-seed twists are an optional accompaniment

ROASTED PROVENÇAL VEGETABLE SOUP

I came across this soup, called Potage Nîmoise, *in the city of Nîmes, the centre of the French vegetable-growing region along the Mediterranean coast. Serve with nutty sesame-seed twists (see box, page 49), if you like.*

1 Omit the cinnamon and the chilli cream. Prepare and salt 1 aubergine (weight about 375 g / 12 oz) as directed.
2 Heat the oven to 180°C (350°F, Gas 4); brush a roasting tin with oil. Arrange the aubergine in the tin.

3 Cut 2 large courgettes (weight about 375 g / 12 oz) lengthwise in half and set the halves, cut-side down, in the tin.

4 Core, halve, and seed 1 large red pepper. Set the halves, cut-side down, in the tin.
5 Brush the surfaces of the vegetables with olive oil and sprinkle with salt and pepper. Bake the vegetables in the heated oven, 25 minutes.
6 Add 250 g (8 oz) plum tomatoes to the tin with the shallots and garlic. Roast the vegetables until soft, about 25 minutes longer, then remove from the oven. Let cool.

7 Meanwhile, strip the leaves from 2 fresh oregano and 5 fresh basil sprigs, reserving 6 basil leaves for garnish. Coarsely chop the leaves.
8 When the roast vegetables are cool enough to handle, squeeze the pulp from the shallots and garlic into a food processor. Cut the courgettes into chunks, add to the food processor, and purée until smooth. If you are using a blender, purée the vegetables in batches. Transfer to a large saucepan.

9 Scoop the flesh from the aubergine halves and put it into the food processor. With a small knife, peel the skin from the red pepper halves. Cut the flesh into chunks and add to the processor.
10 Slip the skins off the tomatoes. Cut each tomato in half and squeeze out the seeds. Add the tomato halves to the food processor and purée until smooth. Transfer to the saucepan.
11 Stir in 1 litre (1²/₃ pints) chicken stock, the lemon juice, the oregano, half of the basil, salt, and pepper and bring to a boil. Simmer, 10 minutes.
12 Serve hot, topped with the remaining chopped basil and the reserved whole leaves.

RED PEPPER SOUP WITH CORIANDER PESTO

🍽 SERVES 6   🥣 WORK TIME 45–55 MINUTES   🍲 COOKING TIME 15–20 MINUTES

EQUIPMENT

wooden spoon

chef's knife

food processor †

slotted spoon

ladle

paper towels

small knife

saucepans

bowls

rubber spatula

chopping board

plastic bag

†blender can also be used

This beautiful red soup has a delicate taste. Red peppers are first roasted under the grill before peeling, which gives them an extra-sweet flavour. The garnish of green pesto, based on fresh coriander and pine nuts, makes a pungent contrast.

GETTING AHEAD

The soup and pesto can be made up to 1 day ahead; keep them separately, covered, in the refrigerator. Just before serving, reheat the soup, but do not let it boil.

metric	SHOPPING LIST	imperial
2	large red peppers, total weight about 500 g (1 lb)	2
500 g	plum tomatoes	1 lb
4	shallots	4
2	garlic cloves	2
30 ml	olive oil, more if needed	2 tbsp
1 litre	vegetable stock (see box, page 124)	1²/₃ pints
10 ml	sugar, more if needed	2 tsp
	juice of ¹/₂ lemon, more if needed	
	salt and pepper	
	For the coriander pesto	
1	bunch of fresh coriander, weighing about 30 g (1 oz)	1
1	bunch of parsley, weighing about 30 g (1 oz)	1
1	garlic clove	1
60 g	pine nuts	2 oz
60 g	freshly grated Parmesan cheese	2 oz
60 ml	olive oil, more if needed	4 tbsp

INGREDIENTS

fresh coriander

red peppers

shallots

olive oil

vegetable stock

plum tomatoes †

parsley

lemon juice

sugar

garlic cloves

Parmesan cheese

pine nuts

†medium tomatoes can also be used

ORDER OF WORK

1 MAKE THE CORIANDER PESTO

2 PREPARE THE VEGETABLES

3 MAKE THE RED PEPPER SOUP

1 MAKE THE CORIANDER PESTO

1 Strip the leaves from the coriander and parsley stalks. You should have about 15 g (½ oz) coriander and 20 g (¾ oz) parsley leaves. Set the flat side of the chef's knife on the garlic clove and strike it with your fist. Discard the skin.

Coriander goes well with red peppers

Parsley modifies pungent flavour of coriander

2 Put the pine nuts, garlic, Parmesan cheese, coriander leaves, parsley leaves, and a little salt and pepper in the food processor or blender and purée until almost smooth.

3 With the blades turning, gradually add the oil. Scrape down the side of the processor bowl from time to time with the rubber spatula.

4 Taste the pesto for seasoning. If it is very thick, work in a little more oil, then transfer the pesto to a bowl. Cover and chill until ready to use.

ANNE SAYS
"Pesto should have a thick and creamy consistency."

Use rubber spatula to scrape side of processor bowl

HOW TO ROAST, PEEL, AND SEED PEPPERS

Grilling peppers makes them easy to peel and adds a smoky flavour.

1 Heat the grill. Set the whole peppers on a rack about 10 cm (4 inches) from the heat. Grill, turning as needed, until the skins blacken and blister, 10–12 minutes. Immediately put the peppers in a plastic bag, close it, and let cool.

2 With a small knife, peel off the skins. Rinse the peppers under cold running water and pat dry with paper towels.

3 Cut around the core of each pepper and pull it out. Cut each pepper lengthwise in half and scrape out the seeds. Cut away the white ribs on the inside.

2 PREPARE THE VEGETABLES

1 Roast, peel, and seed the red peppers (see box, page 55). Set each pepper half, cut-side down, on the chopping board and slice it lengthwise into strips. Gather the strips together in a pile and cut across into dice.

2 Core the tomatoes and score an "x" on the base of each. Immerse them in boiling water until the skins start to split, 8–15 seconds, depending on ripeness. Transfer them at once to cold water. When cool, peel, then halve crosswise. Squeeze out the seeds and coarsely chop each half.

After scalding, skin is easy to remove from tomatoes

3 Peel the shallots and separate into sections if necessary. Slice each shallot horizontally towards the root, leaving the slices attached at the root; then slice vertically, again leaving the root end uncut. Finally, cut across each shallot to make dice.

4 Set the flat side of the chef's knife on top of each garlic clove and strike it with your fist. Discard the skin and finely chop the garlic.

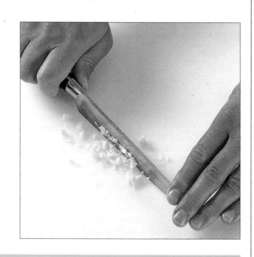

3 MAKE THE RED PEPPER SOUP

1 Heat the oil in a large saucepan, add the shallots and garlic, and sauté, stirring, until soft but not browned, 1–2 minutes.

2 Add the peppers and tomatoes to the saucepan, then stir in the vegetable stock, sugar, salt, and pepper. Bring to a boil. Simmer the soup over medium heat, stirring occasionally, until the vegetables are very soft, 15–20 minutes.

Stir occasionally so vegetables do not stick to bottom of pan

Soup is simmered until vegetables are very soft

3 Remove from the heat and let the soup cool slightly, then purée it in the food processor. The finished consistency should be smooth but not too thick.

ANNE SAYS
"You may have to purée the soup in 2–3 batches."

4 Return the soup to the pan. Add the lemon juice and stir well to combine. Warm the soup over low heat, stirring occasionally. Taste, and add more lemon juice, sugar, salt, and pepper if needed.

Intense red of soup looks stunning in white tureen

 TO SERVE
Transfer the soup to a warmed tureen, then ladle into warmed individual bowls. Top each one with a generous spoonful of pesto and serve at once.

Fragrant green coriander pesto is the ideal partner for red pepper soup

VARIATION

GOLDEN PEPPER SOUP WITH BASIL PESTO

Another stunning colour contrast, this time between the yellow of the soup and the rich green of the basil-based pesto.

1 Omit the tomatoes. Make the pesto as directed, substituting 2 bunches (45g/1½ oz) fresh basil for the fresh coriander and parsley. Reserve 6 small basil sprigs for garnish.
2 Use 4 large yellow peppers (total weight about 1 kg/2 lb) instead of the red peppers; roast, peel, seed, and dice them as directed.
3 Make and purée the soup as directed, adding the juice of 1 lemon.
4 Ladle the soup into warmed bowls and spoon a pattern on each serving with the basil pesto. Garnish each bowl with a sprig of basil and serve immediately.

FRESH GREEN PEA SOUP WITH MINT

🍽 SERVES 4–6 🥣 WORK TIME 1 HOUR* 🍲 COOKING TIME 30 MINUTES**

EQUIPMENT

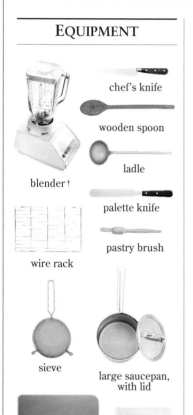

chef's knife

wooden spoon

ladle

blender†

palette knife

pastry brush

wire rack

sieve

large saucepan, with lid

baking sheet

tea towel‡

rolling pin

bowls

chopping board

† food processor can also be used
‡ salad spinner can also be used

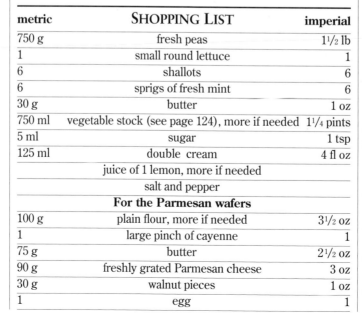

Fresh peas are perfectly complemented by lettuce and fresh mint, as in the classic dish Petits Pois à la française. *Here I make the soup hot, but it is equally good served chilled. Melt-in-the-mouth Parmesan wafers are the ideal accompaniment.*

*plus 45 minutes chilling time for the wafers
**plus 15–18 minutes baking time for the wafers

metric	SHOPPING LIST	imperial
750 g	fresh peas	1½ lb
1	small round lettuce	1
6	shallots	6
6	sprigs of fresh mint	6
30 g	butter	1 oz
750 ml	vegetable stock (see page 124), more if needed	1¼ pints
5 ml	sugar	1 tsp
125 ml	double cream	4 fl oz
	juice of 1 lemon, more if needed	
	salt and pepper	
	For the Parmesan wafers	
100 g	plain flour, more if needed	3½ oz
1	large pinch of cayenne	1
75 g	butter	2½ oz
90 g	freshly grated Parmesan cheese	3 oz
30 g	walnut pieces	1 oz
1	egg	1

INGREDIENTS

fresh peas

Parmesan cheese†

fresh mint

lemon juice

plain flour

vegetable stock

round lettuce

shallots

walnut pieces

egg

cayenne

sugar

butter

double cream

† Gruyère or mature Cheddar cheese can also be used

ORDER OF WORK

1 MAKE THE PARMESAN WAFERS

2 PREPARE THE SOUP INGREDIENTS

3 MAKE THE SOUP

1 MAKE THE PARMESAN WAFERS

Gently knead dough until pliable

1 Sift the flour, cayenne, a little salt, and plenty of pepper onto the work surface. Cut the butter into cubes and rub in with your fingertips until the mixture resembles crumbs.

2 Add the cheese, mix well, and press the dough together firmly with your fingertips. If the cheese is moist, the dough may be sticky. If so, add 30–45 ml (2–3 tbsp) more flour.

3 Lightly flour the work surface. Knead the dough, pushing it with the heel of your hand and pulling it up with your fingers, 2 minutes. Wrap tightly and chill, 30 minutes.

Bunch walnuts with your fingers to make chopping easy

4 Place the walnuts on the chopping board and coarsely chop them with the chef's knife.

5 Roll out the dough to a 12.5 x19 cm (5 x 7½ inch) rectangle, about 1 cm (³/₈ inch) thick. Cut the rectangle into 6 squares, then cut each square diagonally into 2 triangles.

6 Lightly beat the egg with 2.5 ml (½ tsp) salt. Set the triangles on the ungreased baking sheet, then brush with the egg glaze. Sprinkle with the walnuts, pressing them down lightly. Chill, 15 minutes. Meanwhile, heat the oven to 190°C (375°F, Gas 5).

ANNE SAYS
"Instead of walnuts, you can sprinkle the wafers with more grated cheese."

7 Bake in the heated oven until the wafers are golden brown, 15–18 minutes. Let cool, 4–5 minutes, then transfer them to the wire rack to cool completely.

Wafers are fragile when warm so handle them carefully

2 PREPARE THE SOUP INGREDIENTS

Scoop peas from pod with your thumb

1 Shell the peas into a large bowl; there should be about 275 g (9 oz).

ANNE SAYS
"This soup is very good made with 300 g (10 oz) frozen peas. Cook them in the stock, 10–12 minutes."

3 Peel the shallots. Separate into sections if necessary. Set them flat-side down and slice horizontally towards the root, leaving the slices attached at the root. Slice vertically, again leaving the root end uncut, then cut across to make fine dice.

4 Strip the mint leaves from the stalks. Roll up 4–6 leaves and cut them across into fine shreds; reserve for garnish. Leave the remaining mint leaves whole.

2 Pull the lettuce leaves from the core and discard it. Wash the leaves, then dry them in the tea towel. Set 3 leaves aside. Tightly roll the remaining leaves and cut crosswise into coarse shreds. Roll up the 3 reserved leaves and shred finely. Reserve for garnish.

3 MAKE THE SOUP

1 Melt the butter in the saucepan, add the shallots, and sauté, stirring occasionally, until they are soft but not brown, 2–3 minutes.

2 Add the peas. Stir in the stock, sugar, salt, and pepper and bring to a boil. Cover. Simmer until the peas are almost tender, 12–20 minutes.

3 Add the coarsely shredded lettuce leaves and the whole mint leaves. Cover the saucepan and simmer until the peas are tender, 5 minutes longer.

4 Purée the soup in the blender until smooth, in several batches if necessary. Return the soup to the pan.

Blender has helped to emulsify soup so it has creamy consistency

5 Stir 90 ml (3 fl oz) of the cream into the soup, reserving the rest for decoration, and stir in the lemon juice. Bring just to a boil, taste for seasoning, and adjust if necessary.

¡❂¡ TO SERVE
Ladle the soup into warmed soup plates. Decorate each serving with cream (see box, page 42), and top with some of the reserved lettuce and mint. Serve with the Parmesan wafers.

ANNE SAYS
"To serve this soup cold, pour it into a tureen, cover, and chill, at least 3 hours. Add the decoration just before serving."

Cream forms feathered decoration here, but it can also be swirled into soup for a less formal presentation

FRESH GREEN PEA SOUP WITH TARRAGON
In this green pea soup, the distinctive flavour of tarragon takes the place of the more familiar mint.

1 Make the wafers as directed, omitting the walnuts and sprinkling with 2.5 ml (½ tsp) paprika instead.
2 Omit the mint. Prepare the peas and shallots as directed. Cut the lemon in half and squeeze the juice. Coarsely shred all the lettuce leaves. Strip the leaves from 4 sprigs of fresh tarragon with your fingertips.
3 Make the soup as directed, using chicken stock instead of vegetable stock and adding the tarragon leaves with the lettuce.
4 With a slotted spoon, remove 45 g (1½ oz) of the peas and reserve for the garnish.
5 Purée the soup in a blender or food processor until smooth, in several batches if necessary. Finish as directed, using 60 ml (4 tbsp) cream. Serve hot, garnished with the reserved peas and accompanied by the paprika wafers.

——— GETTING AHEAD ———
The soup can be made up to 1 day ahead; keep it, covered, in the refrigerator. Just before serving, reheat the soup and add the garnish. The wafers can be stored up to 1 week in an airtight container, or they can be frozen.

BUTTERNUT SQUASH AND APPLE SOUP

🍽 SERVES 6　🥣 WORK TIME 35–40 MINUTES　☕ COOKING TIME 35–40 MINUTES

EQUIPMENT

small knife

vegetable peeler

large pan, with lid

wooden spoon

large bowl

hand blender †

chef's knife

ladle

chopping board

†standard blender or food processor can also be used

In this richly coloured soup, the sweet taste of butternut squash is perfectly complemented by tart apples – such as Granny Smiths – garlic, and fresh ginger.

GETTING AHEAD

The soup can be made up to 1 day ahead and refrigerated. Just before serving, reheat it on top of the stove. The croûtons can be made up to 1 day ahead and kept tightly wrapped in foil. Warm them, in the foil, in a 180°C (350°F, Gas 4) oven, 8–10 minutes.

INGREDIENTS

butternut squash

tart apples

apple juice

fresh root ginger

garlic clove

chicken stock

onion

butter

lemon juice

fried spiced croûtons (optional)

ANNE SAYS

"Croûtons are a classic garnish for puréed soups. In this recipe I suggest a spicy flavour, but you may like to choose one of the other ideas on page 65."

metric	SHOPPING LIST	imperial
1	onion	1
1	garlic clove	1
2.5 cm	piece of fresh root ginger	1 inch
2–3	butternut squash, total weight about 1.4 kg (3 lb)	2–3
2–3	tart apples, total weight about 375g (12 oz)	2–3
	juice of ½ lemon	
45 g	butter	1½ oz
	salt and pepper	
1 litre	chicken stock (see page 125), more if needed	1²⁄₃ pints
60 ml	apple juice	4 tbsp
	fried spiced croûtons (see box, page 65) for serving (optional)	

ORDER OF WORK

1 PREPARE THE VEGETABLES AND APPLES

2 MAKE THE SOUP

1 PREPARE THE VEGETABLES AND APPLES

1 Peel the onion, leaving a little of the root attached, and cut it lengthwise in half. Lay each onion half on the chopping board and slice horizontally towards the root, leaving the slices attached at the root end.

Onion is cut so root holds together

2 Make a series of vertical cuts through the onion, cutting just to the root but not through it. Finally, cut across the onion to make dice.

ANNE SAYS
"When slicing, use your knuckles to guide the knife."

3 Set the flat side of the chef's knife on top of the garlic clove and strike it with your fist.

4 Discard the skin and finely chop the garlic clove. Peel and finely chop the root ginger (see box, below).

Move knife blade back and forth while chopping garlic

HOW TO PEEL AND CHOP FRESH ROOT GINGER

Fresh root ginger is peeled like a vegetable or thin-skinned fruit, then sliced and chopped. It is important to chop fresh root ginger finely, so the flavour will spread evenly throughout the dish.

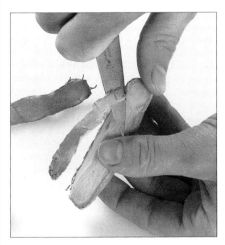

1 With a small knife, peel the skin from the root ginger. Using a chef's knife, slice the ginger, cutting across the fibrous grain.

2 Place the flat side of the chef's knife on the slices of root ginger and crush them by pressing firmly on the blade with your fist.

3 Chop the slices of root ginger as finely as possible, gathering the ginger slices together with your fingers as you chop.

5 Using the vegetable peeler, peel the skin from the butternut squash and discard it.

Skin of butternut squash is soft enough to remove with vegetable peeler

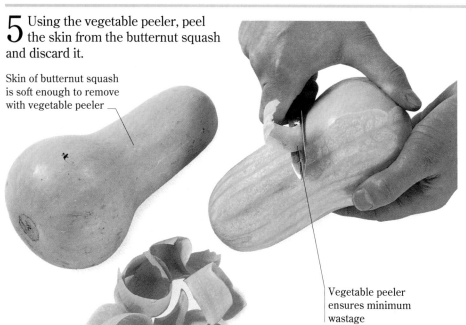

Vegetable peeler ensures minimum wastage

6 Cut the squash lengthwise in half and then into quarters. Cut out and discard the seeds and fibres.

7 With the chef's knife, cut the flesh of the squash crosswise into 2 cm (³/₄ inch) chunks and set aside.

Remove as little apple flesh as possible when cutting around stalk

8 Peel the skin from the apples with the vegetable peeler. With the small knife, cut the flower and stalk ends from the apples.

9 Cut the apples in half, then into quarters. Cut out the cores and cut the apples into 2 cm (³/₄ inch) cubes.

10 Put the apple cubes in the bowl, sprinkle the lemon juice over them, and toss so they are evenly coated.

ANNE SAYS
"The lemon juice will prevent the apples from turning brown."

Work quickly before apples discolour

CROUTON GARNISHES FOR SOUPS

Croûtons are an appealing and crunchy garnish for puréed and creamed soups. They may be fried or oven-toasted in vegetable or olive oil for crispness, in butter if you prefer the flavour, or in a mixture of the two.

FRIED HERB CROUTONS	FRIED SPICED CROUTONS	OVEN-TOASTED CROUTONS

1 Trim the crusts from 3 slices of bread. Cut bread into 1 cm (³/₈ inch) cubes. Finely chop the leaves from 4–6 parsley sprigs. Heat 45–60 ml (3–4 tbsp) oil in a frying pan. Add the cubes and fry, stirring, until brown on all sides, 2–3 minutes.

1 Cube 3 slices of bread as for fried herb croûtons (left). In a small bowl, combine 5 ml (1 tsp) curry powder and 1 large pinch each of ground nutmeg and cardamom, and add pepper to taste. Fry the cubes in hot oil as for fried herb croûtons.

1 Heat the oven to 190°C (375°F, Gas 5). Brush 3 slices of bread with a little oil. Stamp out shapes with an aspic cutter, or cut into cubes.

2 Remove the frying pan from the heat. Lift out the croûtons with a slotted spoon and drain well on paper towels. Toss the croûtons with the chopped parsley.

2 Sprinkle the spice mixture over the croûtons, stir to mix, then at once take the pan from the heat. Lift out the croûtons with a slotted spoon and drain well on paper towels.

2 Place the shapes on an ungreased baking sheet and toast in the heated oven, turning once, until browned on both sides, 5–12 minutes depending on their size.

2 MAKE THE SOUP

1 Melt the butter in the large pan. Add the onion, garlic, and root ginger and cook, stirring, until the onion is soft, 2–3 minutes.

2 Stir the cubes of butternut squash and apple into the pan. Season to taste with salt and pepper.

Apple enhances sweet flavour of squash

3 Pour in the stock and bring to a boil. Cover and simmer gently, stirring occasionally, until the squash and apples are very tender, about 40 minutes. Meanwhile, make the fried spiced croûtons (see box, page 65).

4 Remove the soup from the heat, let cool slightly, then purée it with the hand blender. Alternatively, purée the soup in batches in a standard blender or food processor.

Croûtons should be added to soup at last minute so they keep crisp

5 Reheat the soup, then add the apple juice and stir well to mix. If the soup is too thick, add a little more stock. Taste the soup for seasoning.

🍴 TO SERVE
Ladle the soup into warmed individual bowls. If serving with croûtons, sprinkle a few in the centre of each soup bowl and hand round any extra in a small bowl.

Deep golden colour of soup is echoed by fried spiced croûtons

VARIATION
CURRIED COURGETTE SOUP

Courgettes are soft-skinned with a mild flavour, pepped up here by a warm spicing of curry powder. Choose small courgettes, less than 15 cm (6 inches) long, for this summer soup, garnished here with fried herb croûtons.

1 Omit the squash, fresh ginger, apples, lemon juice, and apple juice. If you like, prepare fried herb croûtons (see box, page 65). Prepare the onion and garlic as directed.

2 Trim 1 kg (2 lb) courgettes and halve lengthwise; cut into 1.25 cm (½ inch) slices. Peel and dice 375 g (12 oz) potatoes.
3 Melt the butter in a large pan. Add the onion and garlic with 30 ml (2 tbsp) curry powder. Cook, stirring, 5 minutes.
4 Add the stock and potatoes. Season to taste with salt and pepper, then simmer, uncovered, 15 minutes. Add the courgettes and simmer, 15–20 minutes.
5 Purée the soup as directed, then taste for seasoning. Ladle the soup into warmed individual bowls and sprinkle with fried herb croûtons, if using.

VARIATION
PUMPKIN AND APPLE SOUP

Here, pumpkin, available in autumn and especially at Hallowe'en, is used with tart apples and fresh ginger to make a deep golden soup with a curry flavour. Dry peeled pumpkin seeds are toasted in the oven to make a simple but attractive garnish.

1 Omit the butternut squash. Prepare the onion, garlic, fresh ginger, and apples as directed.
2 Use a 1.8 kg (4 lb) piece of pumpkin instead of the butternut squash. Cut out the flesh, discarding the seeds and fibres. Cut the flesh into 2 cm (¾ inch) chunks.
3 Make the soup as directed, adding 15 ml (1 tbsp) curry powder with the onion, garlic, and ginger.
4 Make the pumpkin seed garnish: heat the oven to 190°C (375°F, Gas 5).

Place 45 g (1½ oz) dry peeled pumpkin seeds in a small bowl; toss with 15 ml (1 tbsp) vegetable oil. Spread the seeds evenly on a baking sheet and toast until deep golden, stirring as necessary, 6–8 minutes. When cool, toss with a large pinch of salt.
5 Ladle the soup into warmed bowls and garnish each serving with a spoonful of toasted pumpkin seeds. Bagel chips are an appropriate accompaniment.

AMERICAN RED BEAN SOUP

🍽 SERVES 6–8 🥣 WORK TIME 45–55 MINUTES* 🍲 COOKING TIME 2–2¼ HOURS

EQUIPMENT

wooden spoon

ladle

slotted spoon

food processor†

chef's knife

small knife

large pan, with lid

vegetable peeler

colander

bowls

lemon squeezer

medium saucepan

sieve

kitchen string

chopping board

†blender can also be used

INGREDIENTS

dried red kidney beans

smoked bacon knuckle

lemon

tomato purée

parsley

dried hot red chillies

whole cloves

Worcestershire sauce

garlic cloves

onion

carrot

bouquet garni

soured cream

celery

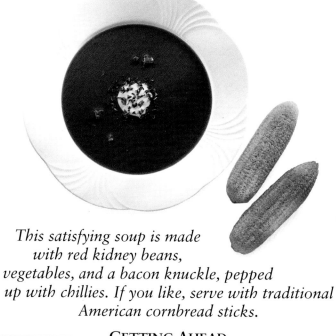

This satisfying soup is made with red kidney beans, vegetables, and a bacon knuckle, pepped up with chillies. If you like, serve with traditional American cornbread sticks.

GETTING AHEAD

The soup can be made up to 3 days ahead; keep it, covered, in the refrigerator. Just before serving, reheat it thoroughly and add the soured cream and parsley decoration.

* plus 8 hours soaking time

metric	SHOPPING LIST	imperial
500 g	dried red kidney beans	1 lb
1	onion	1
2	whole cloves	2
1	large celery stick	1
1	large carrot	1
2	garlic cloves	2
1	lemon	1
1	smoked bacon knuckle, weighing about 500 g (1 lb)	1
2	dried hot red chillies	2
1	bouquet garni (see box, page 70)	1
2 litres	water, more if needed	3½ pints
5 ml	tomato purée	1 tsp
15 ml	Worcestershire sauce, more to taste	1 tbsp
	salt and pepper	
4–6	sprigs of parsley	4–6
125 ml	soured cream	4 fl oz
	cornbread sticks (see box, page 72) for serving (optional)	

ORDER OF WORK

1 **PREPARE THE KIDNEY BEANS**

2 **PREPARE THE OTHER INGREDIENTS**

3 **MAKE THE SOUP**

1 PREPARE THE KIDNEY BEANS

1 Put the red kidney beans into a large bowl. Cover generously with cold water and let soak overnight.

ANNE SAYS
"As an alternative to soaking the beans, put them in a saucepan and cover with cold water. Bring to a boil and let simmer, 1 hour. Drain the beans, rinse with cold water, and drain again."

Water should cover beans during soaking

Dried beans are soaked to rehydrate them before cooking

2 Drain the beans in the colander, rinse under cold running water, and drain again.

2 PREPARE THE OTHER INGREDIENTS

1 Using the small knife, peel the onion and trim off the root and stalk. Stud the onion with the cloves.

2 Peel the strings from the celery with the vegetable peeler. Cut the stick across into 4 cm (1½ inch) pieces, including any leaves.

Celery is left in large chunks as it is puréed after cooking

Guide knife blade with your knuckles

3 Peel and trim the carrot. Using the chef's knife, cut it across into 2.5 cm (1 inch) pieces.

4 Set the flat side of the chef's knife on top of each garlic clove and strike it with your fist. Discard the skin and coarsely chop the garlic.

ANNE SAYS
"Crushing a garlic clove loosens the skin so that it slips off easily."

5 With the vegetable peeler, thinly pare strips of zest from one half of the lemon. Cut the lemon in half and squeeze the juice from both halves.

6 Blanch the bacon: half-fill the saucepan with water, add the bacon and bring to a boil. Boil, 5 minutes. Drain, and rinse with cold water.

7 Trim the hot red chillies, then split lengthwise. Scrape out the seeds and discard them.

ANNE SAYS

"Add fewer or more hot red chillies according to your taste. The seeds are the hottest part, so if you like your soup extra hot, you can leave some of them in."

3 MAKE THE SOUP

Soaked kidney beans soften when simmered

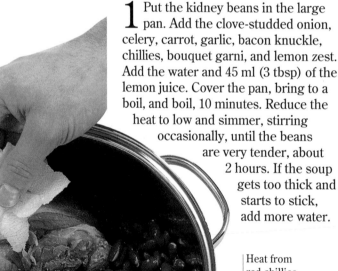

1 Put the kidney beans in the large pan. Add the clove-studded onion, celery, carrot, garlic, bacon knuckle, chillies, bouquet garni, and lemon zest. Add the water and 45 ml (3 tbsp) of the lemon juice. Cover the pan, bring to a boil, and boil, 10 minutes. Reduce the heat to low and simmer, stirring occasionally, until the beans are very tender, about 2 hours. If the soup gets too thick and starts to stick, add more water.

Heat from red chillies permeates soup

HOW TO MAKE A BOUQUET GARNI

This bundle of aromatic flavouring herbs is often required in slowly cooked dishes. It is designed to be easily lifted from the pan and discarded at the end of cooking.

To make a bouquet garni, hold together 2–3 sprigs of fresh thyme, 1 bay leaf, and 5–6 parsley stalks. Wind a piece of white string around the herb stalks and tie them together securely.

Wind string around herb stalks

Always use white untreated string when cooking

2 Lift out the bacon knuckle with the slotted spoon and set aside. Remove the bouquet garni and lemon zest and discard. Set the sieve over a large bowl. Pour the soup into the sieve so the liquid drains into the bowl; reserve the liquid.

Beans and vegetables are separated from liquid before puréeing

Let bacon knuckle cool before handling

3 Remove the cloves from the onion and discard. Put the beans and vegetables, including the onion and the chillies, in the food processor or blender and purée until smooth.

ANNE SAYS
"You may have to do this in 2–3 batches. If the consistency of the purée seems stiff, add a little of the liquid."

4 Using the wooden spoon, press the bean and vegetable purée through the sieve into the pan.

5 Return the reserved liquid to the pan and stir to mix with the purée. Stir in the tomato purée, Worcestershire sauce, salt, and pepper. Bring the soup back to a boil. If it is thin, simmer until it is reduced to the required thickness.

Bacon will add body to soup

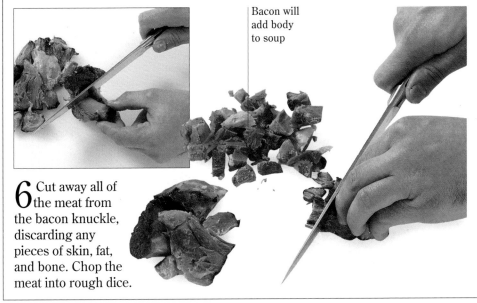

6 Cut away all of the meat from the bacon knuckle, discarding any pieces of skin, fat, and bone. Chop the meat into rough dice.

7 Strip the parsley leaves from the stalks and pile them on the chopping board. With the chef's knife, finely chop the leaves and reserve them for the garnish.

CORNBREAD STICKS

A traditional American complement to bean dishes, cornbread sticks can be made up to 2 days ahead and stored in an airtight container.

🍴 MAKES 14

🥄 WORK TIME 10–12 MINUTES

🍲 BAKING TIME 20–25 MINUTES

SHOPPING LIST

60 g	butter, more for tin	2 oz
150 g	fine yellow cornmeal (polenta)	5 oz
125 g	plain flour	4 oz
15 ml	caster sugar	1 tbsp
5 ml	salt	1 tsp
15 ml	baking powder	1 tbsp
250 ml	milk	8 fl oz
2	eggs	2

1 Heat the oven to 220°C (425°F, Gas 7). Butter 2 corn stick moulds. Melt the butter. Sift the cornmeal, flour, sugar, salt, and baking powder into a bowl and make a well in the centre.

ANNE SAYS
"If you do not have American corn stick moulds, bake the mixture in a 20 cm (8 inch) square cake tin and cut into fingers for serving."

Sifting lightens dry ingredients

2 Whisk the milk and eggs until combined. Pour them into the well in the dry ingredients.

3 Add the melted butter to the well. Mix gently with the wooden spoon until combined.

Mixture should come just to top of moulds

4 Pour the mixture into the corn stick moulds and bake until a skewer inserted in the centre comes out clean, 20–25 minutes. Let cool slightly, unmould, then cool completely on a wire rack.

8 Add the bacon to the soup. Taste; add more Worcestershire sauce, lemon juice, salt, and pepper if needed.

ANNE SAYS
"The soup should be thick and rich, but if it is heavy, add a little water."

🍽 TO SERVE
Ladle the soup into warmed soup plates. Top each serving with a spoonful of soured cream and sprinkle with the chopped parsley. Serve cornbread sticks separately, if you like.

SENATE BLACK BEAN SOUP

Black bean soup has always been a firm favourite in the dining room of the United States Senate in Washington DC. The traditional recipe includes the marrow from beef bones, and sometimes potato is used for thickening.

1 Omit the red kidney beans, cloves, lemon zest, hot red chillies, tomato purée, Worcestershire sauce, and parsley. Use dried black beans; soak as directed.
2 Peel the onion, leaving a little of the root. Cut it lengthwise in half. Set each half, cut-side down, on a chopping board and slice horizontally towards the root, leaving the slices attached at the root end. Then slice vertically, again leaving the root end uncut. Cut across the onion to make dice.

3 Peel the strings from the celery with a vegetable peeler. Cut the stick across into 7.5 cm (3 inch) pieces, then cut each piece lengthwise into 2–3 strips. Stack the strips; cut across into dice.
4 Peel the carrot and trim off the ends. Cut it across into 7.5 cm (3 inch) pieces. Cut each piece lengthwise into slices. Stack the slices and cut each stack into 4–6 strips. Gather the strips together into a pile and cut them crosswise to make medium dice.
5 Set the flat side of a chef's knife on top of each garlic clove and strike it with your fist. Discard the skin and chop the garlic. Blanch, drain, and rinse the bacon knuckle as directed.
6 Heat 15 ml (1 tbsp) vegetable oil in a large pan. Add the onion, celery, and carrot. Sauté until browned, 5 minutes.
7 Add the water, black beans, bacon knuckle, garlic, bouquet garni, salt, and pepper. Bring to a boil and simmer the soup as directed.
8 Strain and purée the soup and dice the bacon knuckle as directed, then return them to the pan. Add 60 ml (4 tbsp) dry sherry, 15 ml (1 tbsp) mustard powder, 1.25 ml (¼ tsp) cayenne, and 30 ml (2 tbsp) lemon juice. Return to a boil. Taste the soup and add more lemon juice, salt, and pepper if needed.
9 Thinly slice 1 lemon. Decorate each plate of soup with lemon slices and top with a spoonful of soured cream.

Soured cream is tangy accompaniment to spicy bean soup

CHICKEN AND SMOKED HAM GUMBO

¶◎⌇ SERVES 6–8 ⌣ WORK TIME 45–55 MINUTES ⚒ COOKING TIME 1–1¼ HOURS

EQUIPMENT

large flameproof casserole

small knife

vegetable peeler

chef's knife

bowls

small glass bowl†

wooden spoon

ladle

colander

slotted spoon

saucepans

chopping board

†ramekin can also be used

This gumbo, from Louisiana, is a fragrant mixture of chicken and vegetables thickened with the sticky juice from sliced okra. The name "gumbo" comes from an African word for okra.

GETTING AHEAD

The gumbo can be made up to 2 days ahead; the flavour will mellow. Keep it, covered, in the refrigerator. Reheat the gumbo thoroughly and cook the rice just before serving.

metric	SHOPPING LIST	imperial
1	onion	1
2	garlic cloves	2
1	small green pepper	1
1	small red pepper	1
1	celery stick	1
500 g	okra	1 lb
250 g	tomatoes	8 oz
1	medium bunch of parsley	1
2–3	sprigs of fresh thyme	2–3
12	chicken thighs, total weight about 1.8 kg (4 lb)	12
250 g	piece of smoked ham	8 oz
75 ml	vegetable oil, more for timbale	2½ fl oz
30 g	plain flour	1 oz
30 ml	tomato purée	2 tbsp
1	bay leaf	1
1 litre	chicken stock (see box, page 125)	1²⁄₃ pints
1.25 ml	cayenne, more if needed	¼ tsp
300 g	long-grain rice	10 oz
	salt and pepper	

INGREDIENTS

smoked ham†

chicken thighs

plain flour

okra

long-grain rice

red pepper

cayenne

garlic cloves

tomatoes

vegetable oil

tomato purée

green pepper

onion

chicken stock

mixed herbs

celery

†spicy sausage can also be used

ORDER OF WORK

1 **PREPARE THE VEGETABLES, HERBS, AND MEAT**

2 **MAKE THE GUMBO**

3 **COOK THE RICE AND FINISH THE GUMBO**

1 PREPARE THE VEGETABLES, HERBS, AND MEAT

When peeling onion, be sure to leave some root to hold it together for chopping

1 Peel the onion and, with the chef's knife, cut it lengthwise in half. Slice each half horizontally towards the root, leaving the slices attached at the root end, then slice vertically, again leaving the root end uncut. Finally, cut across the onion to make dice.

2 Lightly crush each garlic clove with the flat of the chef's knife. Discard the skin and finely chop the garlic. Core, seed, and dice the peppers (see box, page 76).

Choose bright green firm okra without blemishes

To speed slicing, bunch several okra together

3 Peel the strings from the celery with the vegetable peeler and cut across into thin slices.

4 With the chef's knife, trim the stalks and tips from the okra, then cut across into thin slices.

5 Core the tomatoes and score an "x" on the base. Immerse in boiling water until the skins start to split, 8–15 seconds. Transfer to cold water.

6 When the tomatoes are cold, peel off the skins with the small knife. Cut the tomatoes crosswise in half and squeeze out the seeds.

7 Set each half, cut-side down, on the chopping board and slice. Give the slices a half-turn and slice again. Chop the flesh coarsely.

8 Strip the parsley and thyme leaves from their stalks and pile the leaves on the chopping board. With the chef's knife, coarsely chop them.

Pull chicken skin, exerting pressure against knife

Chicken skin is removed to reduce fat in gumbo

9 To skin the chicken thighs, grasp the skin firmly in one hand and pull it away from the meat, cutting with the chef's knife.

10 Cut the ham into 1.25 cm (½ inch) slices, discarding the fat. Stack the slices and cut into strips. Cut across the strips to make dice.

HOW TO CORE, SEED, AND DICE PEPPERS

Peppers are mild members of the capsicum *family, which also includes hot chillies. Their cores and seeds must always be discarded before serving.*

1 Cut around each pepper core and pull it out. Halve the peppers lengthwise, scrape out the seeds, and cut away the white ribs on the inside of the pepper.

2 Set each pepper half, cut-side down, on a work surface and press it down with the heel of your hand to flatten it. This makes the pepper much easier to slice.

3 With a chef's knife, slice each pepper half lengthwise into strips. To make dice, gather the strips together into a neat pile and cut them across to make dice.

2 MAKE THE GUMBO

1 Heat the oil in the casserole. Stir in the flour and cook over low to medium heat, stirring, until the flour is chestnut brown, 10–15 minutes.

! TAKE CARE !
Stir the brown roux constantly so that it does not stick and burn, giving a bitter flavour to the gumbo.

Chestnut brown roux comes with long slow cooking and constant stirring

Stock intensifies flavour of gumbo

3 Stir in the okra, tomatoes, tomato purée, half of the chopped herbs, the bay leaf, chicken stock, cayenne, salt, and pepper and bring to a boil.

2 Add the onion, garlic, green and red peppers, and celery to the casserole. Continue cooking, stirring occasionally, until the vegetables are lightly browned, 8–10 minutes.

! TAKE CARE !
The hot roux will splutter when the vegetables are added.

After long cooking, okra thickens and binds gumbo

4 Add the chicken thighs to the pan, firmly pushing them down into the vegetable mixture. Simmer, stirring occasionally, 30 minutes.

5 Stir the ham cubes into the gumbo and simmer until the chicken thighs are very tender, about 30 minutes longer. Remove the gumbo from the heat.

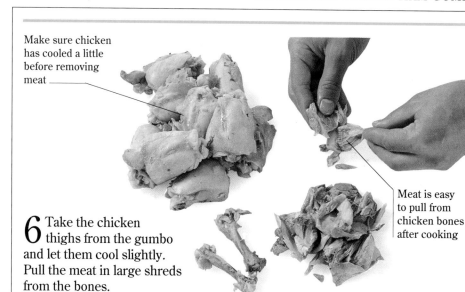

Make sure chicken has cooled a little before removing meat

Meat is easy to pull from chicken bones after cooking

6 Take the chicken thighs from the gumbo and let them cool slightly. Pull the meat in large shreds from the bones.

7 Cut off any sinew from the pieces of chicken and discard. Stir the chicken back into the gumbo.

3 COOK THE RICE AND FINISH THE GUMBO

1 Bring a pan of salted water to a boil, add the rice, and return to the boil. Simmer, stirring occasionally, just until tender, 10–12 minutes. Meanwhile, reheat the gumbo. Drain the rice. Make rice timbales (see box, below) or spoon the rice onto plates.

2 Taste the gumbo for seasoning. Ladle around the rice and sprinkle with the remaining herbs. Serve hot.

HOW TO MAKE A RICE TIMBALE

Moulded rice timbales look very attractive and are simple to make.

Brush a small glass bowl or a ramekin with a little oil or melted butter. Fill with rice and press down lightly. Turn the bowl of rice upside down onto a warm serving plate and lift off the bowl.

Generous strips of chicken add body to gumbo

Boiled rice is traditional accompaniment to gumbo

78

V A R I A T I O N

CHICKEN AND PRAWN GUMBO

Chicken and prawns are favourite ingredients for an authentic gumbo. In this recipe, ground allspice from Jamaica lends an exotic Caribbean note. Okra, which acts as a thickener, is not used here, making this variation of gumbo more of a soup than a stew.

1 Omit the okra and smoked ham. Prepare the remaining vegetables and herbs as directed. Use only 6 chicken thighs (total weight about 1 kg/2 lb).
2 Peel 750 g (1½ lb) large raw prawns with your fingers and devein them (see box, right).

3 Make the gumbo as directed, using all the chopped herbs and adding 5 ml (1 tsp) ground allspice and the juice of ½ lemon with the cayenne. Simmer, 45 minutes. Add the prawns and simmer, 15 minutes longer.

4 Meanwhile, trim 6 spring onions, leaving most of the green tops, and coarsely chop them.
5 Remove the gumbo from the heat, taste for seasoning, and add more cayenne, salt, and pepper if needed. Spoon cooked rice into warmed soup plates and spoon the gumbo on top. Sprinkle with chopped spring onions and serve immediately. Serves 4–6.

ANNE SAYS
"In Louisiana, filé powder – a thickener made from the ground leaves of the sassafras tree – is sometimes added to gumbo. It is hard to find outside the United States, but if you do find some, sprinkle 15–30 ml (1–2 tbsp) onto the gumbo after removing it from the heat: it will thicken at once."

HOW TO PEEL AND DEVEIN PRAWNS

Prawns have a dark intestinal vein along the back that should always be removed before cooking. The tail shell can be left on, if you like.

1 Peel off the shells from the prawns with the tips of your fingers. Discard the shells.

2 Using a small knife, make a shallow cut along the back of each peeled prawn.

3 Gently pull out the intestinal vein that runs along the back of the prawn and discard it.

MONKFISH AND GARLIC SOUP WITH SAFFRON

🍽 SERVES 6–8 🥣 WORK TIME 40–45 MINUTES 🍲 COOKING TIME 25–30 MINUTES

EQUIPMENT

chef's knife

filleting knife

food processor†   large whisk

pastry brush

vegetable peeler

bowls

wooden spoon

ladle

slotted spoon

small knife

colander

baking sheet   large sieve

rubber spatula

saucepans,
1 with lid

serrated knife

paper towels

†blender can also be used

INGREDIENTS

monkfish
fillets   leeks

fresh
chervil†   dry
white
wine   garlic
cloves

mayonnaise

green
peppercorns
in brine

saffron
threads   olive
oil

fish stock

orange

tomatoes   butter

French baguette   onion

†parsley can also be used

Garlic mayonnaise gives a strong punch to this saffron-tinted fish soup, which is finished with a colourful garnish of tomato dice and fresh chervil.

metric	SHOPPING LIST	imperial
750 g	skinned monkfish fillets	1½ lb
1	large onion	1
250 g	leeks	8 oz
6	garlic cloves	6
5 ml	green peppercorns in brine	1 tsp
1	orange	1
30 ml	boiling water	2 tbsp
1	large pinch of saffron threads	1
30 g	butter	1 oz
250 ml	dry white wine	8 fl oz
750 ml	fish stock (see box, page 125)	1¼ pints
	salt	
250 ml	bottled mayonnaise	8 fl oz
	For the croûtes	
1	French baguette, weighing 175–250 g (6–8 oz)	1
30–45 ml	olive oil	2–3 tbsp
	For the garnish	
250 g	tomatoes	8 oz
4–6	sprigs of fresh chervil	4–6

ORDER OF WORK

1 PREPARE THE MONKFISH, VEGETABLES, AND FLAVOURINGS

2 PREPARE THE CROÛTES AND GARNISH

3 MAKE THE SOUP

1 PREPARE THE MONKFISH, VEGETABLES, AND FLAVOURINGS

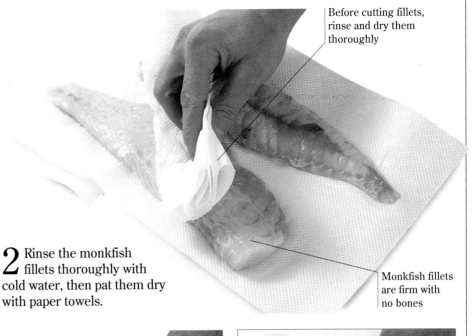

Before cutting fillets, rinse and dry them thoroughly

Monkfish fillets are firm with no bones

1 If necessary, cut away the thin membrane that covers the flesh of the monkfish: cut close to the flesh with the fileting knife and pull the membrane away from the fish with your fingers.

2 Rinse the monkfish fillets thoroughly with cold water, then pat them dry with paper towels.

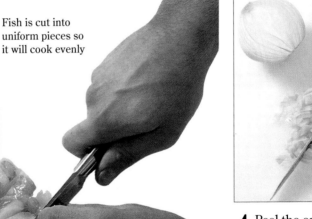

Fish is cut into uniform pieces so it will cook evenly

3 Using the chef's knife, cut the fillets lengthwise into 2–3 strips about 1.25 cm (1/2 inch) wide. Cut the strips across into 1.25 cm (1/2 inch) cubes. Put the cubes into a bowl, cover, and chill while preparing the vegetables and flavourings.

4 Peel the onion, leaving a little of the root attached, and cut it lengthwise in half. Set each half cut-side down and slice horizontally towards the root, leaving the slices attached at the root end. Then slice vertically, again leaving the root end uncut. Cut across to make dice.

5 Using the chef's knife, trim each leek, discarding the root and the tough green top.

6 Slit each leek lengthwise in half, then cut crosswise into 3 mm (1/8 inch) slices. Put the leek slices in the colander, then wash them thoroughly under cold running water. Leave the leeks to drain.

7 Set the flat side of the chef's knife on top of each garlic clove and strike it with your fist to crush the garlic lightly. Discard the skin.

8 Set the flat side of the chef's knife on the green peppercorns and strike it with your fist to crush them.

Crushing green peppercorns releases their flavour

9 With the vegetable peeler, thinly pare strips of zest from the orange, leaving the white pith behind.

White pith is bitter and should be left on orange

Aromatic orange zest is found on surface of peel

10 Pour the boiling water into a small bowl and add the saffron. Let the saffron soak, 10 minutes.

2 PREPARE THE CROUTES AND GARNISH

Olive oil adds flavour to croûtes

2 Lightly brush each side of the bread slices with olive oil. Spread the slices on the baking sheet and bake them in the heated oven until lightly browned, turning once, 10–12 minutes.

1 Heat the oven to 180°C (350°F, Gas 4). Cut the baguette diagonally into thick slices, discarding the ends.

Bread is lightly brushed with olive oil

Tomato cores are removed before peeling

3 Cut the cores from the tomatoes and score an "x" on the base of each with the tip of the small knife. Immerse them in a saucepan of boiling water until the skins start to split, 8–15 seconds depending on ripeness.

4 Using the slotted spoon, transfer the tomatoes at once to a bowl of cold water to stop the cooking. When cool, peel off the skins with the help of the small knife.

5 Put each tomato on the chopping board and cut away the outer layer of flesh, leaving the seeds behind. Cut the flesh into thin strips, then cut across the strips to make neat dice; reserve for garnish.

Follow curve of tomato with knife

6 With your fingertips, strip the chervil sprigs from their stalks and reserve for garnish.

3 MAKE THE SOUP

1 Melt the butter in a large saucepan, add the diced onion and leek slices, and cook them over low heat, stirring occasionally, until very soft but not brown, 5–7 minutes.

2 Stir in the garlic cloves, the saffron with its liquid, orange zest, crushed green peppercorns, wine, stock, and a pinch of salt.

Deep golden colour of saffron is unmistakable

Orange zest enhances flavour of broth

Broth doubles as cooking liquid for monkfish

3 Bring the vegetable and saffron broth to a boil, then cover the saucepan and simmer, 10 minutes.

4 Set the sieve over a bowl and pour the broth into it. Remove and discard the orange zest. Reserve the vegetable mixture. Pour the strained broth back into the saucepan and bring to a simmer.

5 Add the monkfish cubes to the strained broth. Simmer until the fish becomes opaque, 2–3 minutes.

! TAKE CARE !
Do not overcook the monkfish cubes or they will be tough.

6 Take the saucepan from the heat, remove the monkfish with a slotted spoon, and set aside.

7 Put the reserved vegetable mixture into the food processor or blender. Add the mayonnaise to the vegetables and purée until smooth.

Green peppercorns are left in vegetable mixture to add piquant flavour

8 Whisk half of the garlic mayonnaise into the broth. Bring the mixture almost to a boil, stirring constantly.

ANNE SAYS
"Do not boil the soup or it may curdle."

Reheat monkfish cubes at last minute so they do not overcook and toughen

Soup should already be very hot

9 Stir in the monkfish cubes and reheat until very hot, 1–2 minutes. Taste the soup for seasoning.

🍴◉ TO SERVE
Ladle the soup into a warmed tureen and garnish with the diced tomato and chervil sprigs. Pass the croûtes and remaining garlic mayonnaise separately for guests to help themselves.

Extra garlic mayonnaise is served with soup

Chopped tomato adds a splash of colour to this pastel fish soup

MONKFISH, TOMATO, AND GARLIC SOUP

Here, tomatoes and a tomato-garlic mayonnaise turn the soup a delicate pink.

1 Omit the onion, orange, and saffron. Prepare the monkfish, vegetables, and flavourings as directed.
2 Peel and seed 375 g (12 oz) tomatoes as directed. Coarsely chop the tomatoes.
3 Prepare the croûtes as directed. Omit the tomato and chervil garnish. Strip the leaves from 4 sprigs of flat-leaf parsley and pile them on a chopping board. With a chef's knife, coarsely chop the parsley leaves.
4 Make the soup as directed, adding the tomatoes with the leeks. Strain the broth, and purée the vegetables with the mayonnaise as directed, adding 10 ml (2 tsp) tomato purée.
5 Finish the soup as directed, then ladle into warmed soup plates, and sprinkle each one with a little of the coarsely chopped parsley. Serve immediately, accompanied by the croûtes spread with the remaining tomato-garlic mayonnaise.

GETTING AHEAD
The croûtes and the ingredients for the soup can be prepared up to 8 hours ahead and kept, tightly wrapped, in the refrigerator. Prepare the garnish and make the soup just before serving.

GERMAN SPLIT PEA SOUP

🍽 SERVES 6–8 🥣 WORK TIME 35–40 MINUTES 🍲 COOKING TIME 2–2¼ HOURS

EQUIPMENT

large flameproof
casserole, with lid

small
knife

vegetable
peeler

chef's knife

slotted spoon

sieve

wooden spoon

small bowl

ladle

chopping board

*A hearty and satisfying soup –
ideal for a chilly day. Split peas and lots of
vegetables give the soup body, and the broth is
richly flavoured with a smoked bacon knuckle
and beer. Frankfurter slices, mustard, and
chopped parsley add the finishing touch.*

GETTING AHEAD

The soup can be made up to 2 days ahead and the flavour
will mellow; keep it, covered, in the refrigerator. Just before
serving, reheat the soup and add the frankfurters, mustard,
and parsley.

metric	SHOPPING LIST	imperial
2	large onions	2
250 g	carrots	8 oz
250 g	potatoes	8 oz
250 g	swede	8 oz
2	celery sticks	2
250 g	dried yellow split peas	8 oz
3	whole cloves	3
1	bouquet garni, made with 5–6 parsley stalks, 2–3 sprigs of fresh thyme, and 1 bay leaf	1
1	smoked bacon knuckle, weighing about 500 g (1 lb)	1
1 litre	water, more if needed	1²/₃ pints
500 ml	light ale	16 fl oz
	salt and pepper	
250 g	frankfurters	8 oz
1	medium bunch of parsley	1
5 ml	mustard powder	1 tsp

INGREDIENTS

frankfurters†

yellow split
peas

swede

smoked
bacon knuckle

potatoes

parsley

celery

onions

light ale

bouquet
garni

carrots

whole
cloves

mustard
powder

†cooked bratwurst or knackwurst
can also be used

ORDER OF WORK

1 PREPARE THE
INGREDIENTS

2 MAKE THE SOUP

1 PREPARE THE INGREDIENTS

1 Peel the onions and trim the tops, leaving a little of the roots. Chop into small dice (see box, page 88).

2 Peel and trim the carrots. Cut each carrot across into 5 cm (2 inch) pieces. Cut each piece lengthwise into 5 mm ($^1/_4$ inch) slices. Stack the slices and cut into 4–6 strips. Gather the strips together and cut into dice.

3 Peel the potatoes. With the chef's knife, cut a thin slice from each potato so it sits flat. Cut the potatoes lengthwise into 5 mm ($^1/_4$ inch) slices. Stack the slices and cut each stack into 5 mm ($^1/_4$ inch) strips. Gather the strips into a pile and cut crosswise into dice.

4 Peel the swede. Cut it into 5 mm ($^1/_4$ inch) slices, then into strips and into dice, as for the potatoes.

5 Peel the strings from the celery with the vegetable peeler. Cut the sticks lengthwise into 5 mm ($^1/_4$ inch) strips, then crosswise into dice.

Use your thumb to steady vegetable peeler

Peeling outside of celery removes tough strings

6 Put the split peas into the sieve and rinse thoroughly under cold running water. Pick over and discard any stones. Leave the split peas to drain.

ANNE SAYS

"If you soak the split peas in cold water for 8 hours, the cooking time for the soup will be reduced by about 1 hour."

HOW TO CHOP AN ONION

The size of dice when chopping an onion depends on the initial slices. For a standard size, make slices 5 mm (¼ inch) thick. For finely chopped onions, slice very thinly.

1 Place the onion on a chopping board and, holding it firmly with one hand, cut it lengthwise in half with a chef's knife.

2 Lay each onion half, cut-side down, on the chopping board. Holding the onion half steady, slice it horizontally towards the root, leaving the slices attached at the root end.

3 Slice the onion vertically, again leaving the root end uncut. Finally, cut across the onion to make neat dice.

2 MAKE THE SOUP

1 Tuck the cloves into the string tied around the bouquet garni. Combine the diced vegetables and split peas in the casserole and add the bacon knuckle, water, bouquet garni, beer, salt, and pepper. Bring to a boil. Skim off the scum that rises to the surface, then cover, and simmer until the split peas are very tender, 2–2¼ hours. Stir the soup from time to time and add more water if it seems too thick.

Beer adds depth of flavour to soup

2 Meanwhile, using the chef's knife, cut the frankfurters into 1.25 cm (½ inch) diagonal slices.

3 Strip the parsley leaves from the stalks and pile the leaves on the chopping board. With the chef's knife, finely chop them.

4 Put the mustard powder into the small bowl. Spoon in 15–30 ml (1–2 tbsp) of the hot soup liquid and stir well until the mustard powder has dissolved completely. Reserve.

5 Remove the bacon knuckle and bouquet garni from the casserole. Let cool slightly, then pull off any meat and chop coarsely, discarding any skin and fat. Return the meat to the soup.

6 Add the frankfurter slices and cook gently without boiling until they are heated through, 3–5 minutes.

ANNE SAYS
"The consistency of the soup should be thick and rich, but if it is heavy, stir in more water."

7 Stir in the mustard mixture and most of the chopped parsley. Taste the soup for seasoning and adjust if necessary.

Stir in chopped parsley just before serving so it stays green

¶◉¶ TO SERVE
Ladle the soup into warmed soup plates and sprinkle a little of the remaining chopped parsley on each one. Serve immediately, with pumpernickel or dark rye bread, if you like.

Frankfurters
bolstered with bacon and split peas make a warming soup for a winter's day

GREEN SPLIT PEA AND BACON SOUP

A subtle spicing of ground coriander and cloves lifts the flavour of this main-dish soup.

1 Omit the bacon knuckle, frankfurters, cloves, and mustard. Prepare the vegetables as directed, using green split peas instead of yellow split peas.
2 Make the soup as directed, adding 2.5 ml (1/2 tsp) ground coriander and a pinch of ground cloves with the salt and pepper.
3 After about 45 minutes of cooking, add a 500 g (1 lb) piece of lean bacon.
4 When the split peas are very tender, remove the bacon and cut it into dice, discarding any rind. Remove and discard the bouquet garni.
5 Return the diced bacon to the soup and stir in all the chopped parsley. Taste for seasoning. Serve hot.

Pumpernickel bread
is an appropriate accompaniment to a German-style soup

TURKISH MEATBALL SOUP

🍽 SERVES 6 🥄 WORK TIME 40–45 MINUTES 🍲 COOKING TIME 20–30 MINUTES

EQUIPMENT

chef's knife

whisk

large metal spoon

food processor †

slotted spoon

salad spinner ‡

ladle

bowls

vegetable peeler

lemon squeezer

frying pan

chopping board

saucepans

sieve

palette knife

aluminium foil

† blender can also be used
‡ tea towel can also be used

Fine strips of spinach, carrot, and celery, and tiny spiced lamb meatballs give a pleasing contrast of colours and textures to this Middle Eastern soup. In the traditional Turkish manner, egg yolks and lemon juice are used for thickening the soup, as well as to enrich and sharpen the flavour. Fresh dill completes the presentation.

GETTING AHEAD

The meatballs and vegetables can be prepared up to 8 hours ahead and kept, covered, in the refrigerator. Make the soup just before serving.

metric	SHOPPING LIST	imperial
1	large carrot	1
1	celery stick	1
175 g	fresh spinach leaves	6 oz
3–4	sprigs of fresh dill	3–4
2	lemons	2
1.5 litres	chicken stock (see box, page 125)	2¹⁄₃ pints
3	egg yolks	3
	salt and pepper	
	For the meatballs	
4	spring onions	4
2	slices of white bread	2
250 g	lean minced lamb	8 oz
1.25 ml	ground cinnamon	¹⁄₄ tsp
1	large pinch of ground allspice	1
1	egg	1

INGREDIENTS

minced lamb

fresh spinach

egg yolks

spring onions

fresh dill

white bread

lemons

celery

ground cinnamon

egg

chicken stock

carrot

ground allspice

ORDER OF WORK

1 PREPARE THE MEATBALLS

2 PREPARE THE VEGETABLES AND HERBS

3 MAKE THE SOUP

1 PREPARE THE MEATBALLS

1 Trim the spring onions, leaving most of the green tops. Slice lengthwise into thin strips. Chop the strips finely. Trim and discard the crusts from the bread. Cut the bread into chunks and work in the food processor to form crumbs.

Spring onions add mild onion flavour

2 Put the minced lamb into a bowl and add the spring onions, breadcrumbs, cinnamon, allspice, salt, and pepper.

Fresh breadcrumbs lighten meatballs

3 Squeeze the ingredients together with your fingers to mix evenly. Add the egg and mix in well.

ANNE SAYS
"*Alternatively, you can work the meatball ingredients together in a food processor, using the pulse button.*"

Meatballs are shaped into even-sized pieces

4 Heat the frying pan, add a little of the meatball mixture, and fry, 1–2 minutes. Taste, and add more spices, salt, and pepper to the remaining mixture if needed.

Wet hands stop mixture from sticking

5 With wet hands, break off pieces of the meat mixture and roll between your palms into balls the size of large cherries. Put the meatballs on a dampened plate, cover, and refrigerate until ready to use.

2 PREPARE THE VEGETABLES AND HERBS

1 Peel and trim the carrot, then cut it into fine julienne strips with the chef's knife (see box, below).

2 Peel the strings from the celery stick with the vegetable peeler. Cut the stick into fine julienne strips (see box, below).

3 Discard the tough ribs and stalks from the spinach leaves, then wash them thoroughly in several changes of cold water. Dry them in the salad spinner or on a tea towel.

HOW TO CUT VEGETABLES INTO JULIENNE STRIPS

Vegetables cut into julienne strips the size of fine matchsticks are quick to prepare and cook. The principle is much the same for carrots, celery, turnips, or courgettes – whatever your selection.

Slice straight down to board

1 Peel and trim, then cut long vegetables into pieces 5–7.5 cm (2–3 inches) long, using a chef's knife.

2 For rounded vegetables, cut a thin strip from one side so that the vegetable can lie flat on the chopping board as you slice.

3 Holding the vegetable steady with one hand, cut it lengthwise into thin vertical slices.

4 Stack the slices and cut into fine strips, keeping the tip of the knife on the board as you slice, and guiding it with your curled fingers. Use a strip as a guide for length when cutting other vegetables.

Sharp knife is essential for fine julienne strips

4 Take a few leaves of spinach at a time, stack them, and roll them up tightly. Cut across into thin slices to make fine shreds.

When slicing, use your knuckles to guide knife blade

Roll spinach leaves tightly so they are easy to shred

Spinach will give deep colour to soup

5 Strip the dill leaves from the stalks and pile the leaves on the chopping board. Chop the leaves coarsely.

6 Cut the lemons in half and squeeze the juice. Strain into a measuring cup; there should be 90 ml (3 fl oz).

3 MAKE THE SOUP

1 Pour the chicken stock into a large saucepan and heat it through until it is boiling. Add the meatballs to the stock.

Skim stock frequently so soup is not greasy

2 Simmer the meatballs gently in the stock, skimming occasionally, until they are firm and thoroughly cooked, 8–10 minutes.

3 With the slotted spoon, lift the meatballs out of the stock and cover with foil to keep warm. Strain the stock into a clean saucepan.

4 Add the carrot and celery julienne strips to the strained stock and simmer, stirring occasionally, just until tender, 2–3 minutes.

Heat of stock wilts and cooks spinach

5 Take the pan from the heat and stir in the shredded spinach. Taste the soup for seasoning.

6 In a medium bowl, whisk the egg yolks with half of the lemon juice until the mixture is frothy and slightly thickened, about 1 minute.

7 Add a ladleful of the soup to the egg yolk and lemon mixture and whisk well together. Whisk in a second ladleful of soup.

8 Stir the soup and egg yolk mixture back into the remaining soup in the pan.

Combining some hot soup with egg and lemon mixture helps prevent curdling

9 Add the meatballs to the pan and reheat the soup gently to just below boiling point.

! TAKE CARE !
Do not let the soup boil or the egg yolks may curdle.

Warm meatballs briefly in soup before serving

10 Stir in the chopped dill and 15 ml (1 tbsp) of the remaining lemon juice. Taste, and add more lemon juice, salt, and pepper if needed.

 TO SERVE
Transfer the soup to a warmed tureen and ladle it into warmed soup plates.

Carrot julienne makes bright contrast to spinach and dill

V A R I A T I O N

EGG AND LEMON SOUP WITH COURGETTES

Rice and courgettes give body to this egg yolk and lemon soup, finished with a decoration of lemon and mint.

1 Omit the meatballs, spinach, carrot, celery, and dill.
2 Heat the stock to boiling in a large pan, add 60 g (2 oz) rice, and simmer, covered, until tender, 10–12 minutes.
3 Meanwhile, trim but do not peel 2 medium courgettes (total weight 250 g/8 oz) and cut them into julienne strips.
4 Strip the leaves from 4–5 coriander sprigs and 4–5 mint sprigs. Pile the leaves together and finely chop them.
5 Add the courgette strips to the soup and simmer just until they are tender, about 1 minute.
6 Squeeze the juice from 1 lemon. Whisk the egg yolks with half of the lemon juice, then whisk into the soup as directed.
7 Take from the heat, stir in the coriander and mint, and taste for seasoning, adding more lemon juice, salt, and pepper if needed. Serve the soup at once, decorated with lemon slices and mint, if you like.

HEARTY BEAN AND VEGETABLE SOUP

🍽 SERVES 6–8　🥄 WORK TIME 45–50 MINUTES*　🍲 COOKING TIME 2½–2¾ HOURS

EQUIPMENT

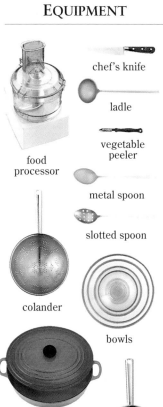

chef's knife

ladle

vegetable peeler

food processor

metal spoon

slotted spoon

colander

bowls

large flameproof casserole, with lid

medium saucepan

kitchen scissors

baking sheet

paper towels

chopping board

serrated knife

Substantial enough for a main course, this soup is good all the year round. Add more vegetables, or omit those you cannot find, according to the season.

GETTING AHEAD

The soup can be made up to 3 days ahead; keep it, covered, in the refrigerator and reheat it thoroughly before serving. Make the sun-dried tomato croûtes just before serving.

*plus 8 hours soaking time

INGREDIENTS

salt pork

turnips

leeks

potatoes

haricot beans

carrots

butter

chicken stock

white cabbage

bouquet garni

garlic

French beans

celery

small French baguette

sun-dried tomatoes

metric	SHOPPING LIST	imperial
200 g	haricot beans	7 oz
250 g	piece of salt pork belly	8 oz
1	bouquet garni, made with 5–6 parsley stalks, 2–3 sprigs of fresh thyme, and 1 bay leaf	1
3 litres	chicken stock (see box, page 125)	4²/₃ pints
500 g	leeks	1 lb
175 g	turnips	6 oz
250 g	carrots	8 oz
250 g	potatoes	8 oz
3	large celery sticks	3
½	head of white cabbage, weighing about 250 g (8 oz)	½
125 g	French beans	4 oz
2	garlic cloves	2
	salt and pepper	
For the sun-dried tomato croûtes		
2	sun-dried tomatoes packed in oil	2
60 g	butter	2 oz
1	small French baguette, weighing 175–200 g (6–8 oz)	1

ORDER OF WORK

1 PREPARE THE HARICOT BEANS AND SALT PORK

2 PREPARE THE VEGETABLES AND SIMMER THE SOUP

3 MAKE THE CROÛTES

4 FINISH THE SOUP

1 PREPARE THE HARICOT BEANS AND SALT PORK

1 Put the beans into a bowl. Cover generously with cold water and let soak overnight.

2 Rinse the salt pork, put it into the saucepan, and cover with cold water. Bring to a boil and simmer, 10 minutes. Drain the salt pork thoroughly.

ANNE SAYS
"This will remove excess salt from the pork."

3 Drain the beans in the colander, rinse under cold running water, and drain again.

ANNE SAYS
"As an alternative to soaking the beans, put them in a saucepan and cover with water. Bring to a boil and let simmer, 1 hour. Drain the beans, rinse with cold water, and drain again."

Chicken stock adds hearty flavour to beans and salt pork

4 Put the beans, salt pork, and bouquet garni into the casserole and add all but 500 ml (16 fl oz) of the chicken stock. Bring to a boil, and boil, 10 minutes. Cover the pan and simmer, skimming if necessary, 1 hour. Meanwhile, prepare the vegetables.

2 PREPARE THE VEGETABLES AND SIMMER THE SOUP

2 Place each leek half, cut-side down, on the chopping board, fanning it slightly so it lies flat. Cut across into 5 mm (¼ inch) slices.

Only tender parts of leeks are used

1 Trim the leeks, discarding the roots and tough green tops. Slit the leeks lengthwise in half and wash them thoroughly under cold running water.

HOW TO DICE VEGETABLES

Sharp knives are essential when dicing root vegetables, such as potatoes, carrots, and turnips. Grasp the knife firmly with all four fingers wrapped around the handle, and use your free hand to steady the vegetable and guide the knife blade as you cut.

Keep fingers out of knife blade's way

1 Peel or trim vegetable; then square off sides if necessary. Cut into 1.25 cm (¹/₂ inch) slices.

2 Stack the slices together and cut downwards through them to make 1.25 cm (¹/₂ inch) strips.

3 Gather the strips together into a pile and cut them crosswise to produce even 1.25 cm (¹/₂ inch) dice.

3 Peel the turnips, carrots, and potatoes and cut them into 1.25 cm (¹/₂ inch) dice (see box, above).

ANNE SAYS
"If not using the cut turnips and potatoes at once, put them into cold water so they do not discolour before cooking."

Carrot strips are cut into neat dice

Cut vegetables into dice of equal size so they cook evenly

4 Peel the strings from the celery sticks with the vegetable peeler. Cut the sticks across into 7.5 cm (3 inch) pieces, then cut each piece lengthwise into 2–3 sticks. Stack the sticks and cut across into medium dice.

5 Trim the cabbage, discard any wilted leaves, and cut into quarters. With the chef's knife, cut a wedge around the core and remove it.

6 Set the cabbage flat on the chopping board and cut it into the finest possible shreds. Discard any coarse stalks.

Beans are cut into even-sized pieces

7 With the chef's knife, trim the ends of the French beans and cut them crosswise into 1.25 cm (½ inch) pieces.

8 Set the flat side of the chef's knife on top of each garlic clove and strike it with your fist. Discard the skin and finely chop the garlic.

9 Add all of the prepared vegetables and the garlic to the pork and beans. Season with salt and pepper.

10 Add the remaining chicken stock to the soup and bring back to a boil.

Add enough stock to vegetables so they are completely covered

Vegetables give variety of colour and texture to soup

11 Cover the casserole and simmer until the pork and vegetables are very tender, about 1½ hours longer. About 20 minutes before the end of cooking, make the sun-dried tomato croûtes (see page 100).

3 MAKE THE CROUTES

1 Heat the grill. Remove the sun-dried tomatoes from the jar and pat dry with paper towels.

Sun-dried tomatoes are dried on paper towels before cutting

2 With the scissors, cut the tomatoes into small pieces and put them into the food processor.

3 Add the butter to the food processor and purée until the tomatoes are finely chopped and evenly mixed with the butter. Season with pepper to taste.

4 Using the serrated knife, cut the baguette into 1.25 cm (½ inch) slices on the diagonal, discarding the ends.

Tomato butter makes pungent topping for toasted croûtes

5 Arrange the slices of bread in one layer on the baking sheet and toast on one side under the grill until lightly browned, 2–3 minutes.

6 Turn the bread slices untoasted-side up and spread with the tomato butter. Grill until golden brown, 2–3 minutes.

Butter melts and croûtes become crisp when grilled

4 FINISH THE SOUP

1 Discard the bouquet garni. Lift out the piece of salt pork from the casserole and let it cool slightly.

Meaty part of salt pork adds body to soup

2 Cut the pork into thick slices, discarding any rind. Stack the slices and cut them into strips. Cut the strips into cubes. Put the salt pork back into the soup, bring the soup just back to a boil, and taste for seasoning.

ANNE SAYS
"For a lighter soup, serve without the salt pork."

🍽 TO SERVE
Ladle the soup into 6–8 warmed soup bowls. Serve the croûtes separately.

Sun-dried tomato croûtes add a contemporary touch

Vegetables, beans, and salt pork combine to make a substantial dish

---

V A R I A T I O N

VEGETABLE AND NOODLE SOUP

This light vegetable soup contains courgettes, tomatoes, and vermicelli.

1 Omit the salt pork, haricot beans, cabbage, and potatoes. Prepare the remaining vegetables as directed. Using only 2.5 litres (4 pints) stock, simmer the vegetables as directed, 30 minutes.

2 Cut 250 g (8 oz) courgettes into 1.25 cm (½ inch) dice (see box, page 98), including the skin.

3 Cut the cores from 250 g (8 oz) tomatoes and score an "x" on the base of each with the tip of a small knife. Immerse in boiling water until the skins start to split, 8–15 seconds, depending on their ripeness. Transfer to cold water. When cool, peel off the skins. Cut the tomatoes crosswise in half and squeeze out the seeds, then chop each half.

4 Add the courgettes and tomatoes to the soup and simmer until the vegetables are very tender, about 25 minutes longer.

5 Stir in 125 g (4 oz) vermicelli and continue simmering until it is just tender, 4–5 minutes.

6 Finish the soup as directed and serve with sun-dried tomato croûtes, if you like. Serves 6.

VICHYSSOISE

🍽 SERVES 8 🥄 WORK TIME 35–40 MINUTES* 🍲 COOKING TIME 35–40 MINUTES

EQUIPMENT

blender†

chef's knife

small knife

vegetable peeler

wooden spoon

ladle

sieve

large pan, with lid

colander

chopping board

bowls

†food processor can also be used

This must be one of the most celebrated and elegant of cold soups. It was created by Louis Diat in the 1920s when he was chef at the Ritz-Carlton Hotel in New York. Inspired by memories of his mother's cooking, he added cream to a homely leek and potato soup, served it chilled, and created a masterpiece. It is named after the French spa town of Vichy, near Diat's childhood home.

GETTING AHEAD

The soup can be made up to 1 day ahead; keep it, covered, in the refrigerator.

* plus at least 3 hours chilling time

metric	SHOPPING LIST	imperial
625 g	leeks	1¼ lb
1	onion	1
750 g	potatoes	1½ lb
30 g	butter	1 oz
	salt and pepper	
1 litre	chicken stock (see page 125), more if needed	1⅔ pints
500 ml	milk	16 fl oz
250 ml	single cream	8 fl oz
250 ml	double cream	8 fl oz
1	medium bunch of chives	1

INGREDIENTS

leeks

potatoes

onion

chives

single cream

milk

chicken stock

double cream

butter

ORDER OF WORK

1 PREPARE THE VEGETABLES

2 MAKE AND CHILL THE SOUP

1 PREPARE THE VEGETABLES

Use your
knuckles
to guide
knife blade

1 Trim the leeks,
discarding the roots and the
tough green tops; you should have
about 375 g (12 oz) white leeks
altogether. Using the chef's knife,
slit the leeks lengthwise in half.

Leeks are mildest
members of
onion family

2 Place each leek half, cut-side down,
on the chopping board and cut
crosswise into 3 mm (1/8 inch) slices.

3 Wash the sliced leeks thoroughly
in a bowl of cold water, then lift
them out, and drain in the colander.

ANNE SAYS
*"Leeks are often gritty. Preparing and
washing them in this way ensures that
the grit is left in the water."*

4 Peel the onion, leaving a
little of the root attached,
and cut it lengthwise in half
through root and stalk.

5 Lay each onion half, cut-side down,
on the chopping board. Holding
the onion firmly, cut across into thin
slices. Discard the root.

6 Peel the
potatoes and
cut them in half. Lay
each half on the chopping
board, cut-side down, and
thinly slice. Drop the slices
at once into a bowl of cold
water to prevent them
from discolouring.

Potato halves are
placed cut-side down
to steady them

2 MAKE AND CHILL THE SOUP

Washed leeks are thoroughly drained in colander

1 Melt the butter in the large pan, add the onion, leeks, salt, and pepper and cook, stirring occasionally, until soft but not brown, 7–10 minutes.

! TAKE CARE !
If the vegetables start to brown they will discolour and spoil the look of the finished soup.

Onions and leeks are softened in butter before adding potatoes

2 Drain the potato slices in the colander and then immediately transfer them to the large pan.

3 Add the stock and bring to a boil. Cover and simmer, stirring occasionally, until the potatoes are very tender when pierced with the tip of the small knife, about 30 minutes.

ANNE SAYS
"Leeks are fibrous so it is important to strain soup after puréeing."

Pressing soup through sieve removes all fibrous matter

4 Purée the soup until smooth, in 2 or 3 batches if necessary, in the blender or food processor.

5 Work the soup through the sieve, using the wooden spoon, to remove any leek fibres.

6 Return the soup to the pan and stir in the milk and single cream. Bring the soup just to a simmer, then take from the heat.

! TAKE CARE !
Do not boil the vichyssoise or it may curdle.

Milk and single cream are stirred into leek and potato purée

7 Stir in the double cream and taste for seasoning. Pour the soup into a bowl and let it cool. Cover, and chill thoroughly, at least 3 hours.

8 Stack the chives in a pile on the chopping board and, using the chef's knife, finely chop them.

¶◎¶ TO SERVE
Stir half of the chopped chives into the soup and taste again for seasoning. If the soup is too thick, stir in more stock. Ladle into chilled soup plates. Garnish each serving with a sprinkling of the remaining chives.

Chopped chives
highlight the flavour of vichyssoise

V A R I A T I O N

CHILLED FENNEL, LEEK, AND POTATO SOUP

The pleasant liquorice taste of fennel adds another dimension to creamy leek and potato soup.

1 Omit the double cream and the chopped chives. Increase the single cream to 500 ml (16 fl oz). Prepare the vegetables as directed, using 300 g (10 oz) leeks, 1 small onion, and 750 g (1½ lb) potatoes.
2 Prepare 2 fennel bulbs (total weight about 625 g/1¼ lb): trim the stalks and roots, discarding any tough outer pieces. Reserve the feathery tops for garnish. Cut each fennel bulb lengthwise into quarters. Set each quarter flat on a chopping board and thinly slice.
3 Make the soup as directed, adding the sliced fennel with the onion and leeks. Add 2.5 ml (½ tsp) fennel seeds with the potatoes.
4 Serve the soup well chilled, garnished with the feathery tops from the fennel bulbs. Serves 8–10.

Creamy soup
is velvety smooth

CHILLED GUACAMOLE SOUP

 SERVES 6   WORK TIME 25–30 MINUTES*   COOKING TIME 1–2 MINUTES

EQUIPMENT

chef's knife

hand blender †

small saucepan

slotted spoon

small knife

ladle

bowls

grater

lemon squeezer

rubber gloves

cling film

baking sheet

chopping board

†food processor or standard blender can also be used

INGREDIENTS

avocados

limes

Tabasco sauce

tortilla chips

tequila †

soured cream

chicken stock

fresh hot red chilli

tomatoes

mild Cheddar cheese

fresh coriander

†vodka can also be used

The Mexican dip, guacamole, is the inspiration for this piquant chilled soup. Avocados and soured cream provide the smooth base, which is spiked with lime juice, tequila, and Tabasco sauce. Diced tomatoes and chopped fresh coriander make the colourful garnish. Tortilla chips topped with cheese and chilli are an appropriate accompaniment.

GETTING AHEAD

The soup can be made up to 4 hours ahead and kept, in a covered non-metallic container, in the refrigerator. Make the cheese-chilli tortilla chips and add the tomato and fresh coriander garnish just before serving.

* plus at least 1 hour chilling time

metric	SHOPPING LIST	imperial
2	limes, more if needed	2
2	large avocados, total weight about 500 g (1 lb)	2
250 ml	cold chicken stock (see page 125), more if needed	8 fl oz
250 ml	soured cream	8 fl oz
15 ml	tequila	1 tbsp
1	dash of Tabasco sauce, more if needed	1
	salt and pepper	
250 g	tomatoes	8 oz
6	sprigs of fresh coriander	6
For the cheese-chilli tortilla chips		
1	fresh hot red chilli	1
60 g	mild Cheddar cheese	2 oz
125 g	plain tortilla chips	4 oz

ORDER OF WORK

1 MAKE AND CHILL THE SOUP

2 PREPARE THE GARNISH

3 PREPARE THE CHEESE-CHILLI TORTILLA CHIPS AND FINISH THE SOUP

1 MAKE AND CHILL THE SOUP

1 Cut the limes in half and squeeze the juice in the lemon squeezer; there should be 75 ml (2½ fl oz) juice.

2 With the chef's knife, cut lengthwise around each avocado through to the stone. Twist the avocados with both hands to loosen the halves, then pull them apart.

Avocado halves slide apart when twisted

3 With a chopping movement, embed the blade of the chef's knife in each stone and lift it out of the avocado half. Alternatively, scoop out the avocado stone with a spoon.

When stone comes out cleanly, it is a sign that avocado is ripe

4 With a spoon, scoop the avocado flesh from the skins and put it in a large non-metallic bowl.

Soured cream lightens soup to pale green

Hand blender is simple to operate

5 Add the lime juice and stock, and purée with the hand blender until smooth. You can also purée the soup in batches using a food processor or standard blender.

ANNE SAYS
"Work quickly so there is no time for the avocado to discolour."

6 Add the soured cream, tequila, Tabasco sauce, salt, and pepper and purée again briefly to mix. Taste, and add more lime juice, Tabasco, salt, and pepper if needed. Cover the soup tightly and refrigerate until well chilled, at least 1 hour; it should be very cold.

2 PREPARE THE GARNISH

Fresh coriander is classic combination with avocado

1 Cut the cores from the tomatoes and score an "x" on the base of each tomato. Immerse in boiling water until the skins start to split, 8–15 seconds depending on their ripeness. Using the slotted spoon, transfer the tomatoes at once to a bowl of cold water. When cool, peel off the skin.

2 With the small knife, cut the tomatoes into sections and cut away the seeds. Place the pieces of tomato, cut-sides down, on the chopping board and cut into dice.

3 Strip the leaves from the coriander sprigs with your fingers and pile them on the chopping board. Using the chef's knife, coarsely chop the leaves.

3 PREPARE THE CHEESE-CHILLI TORTILLA CHIPS AND FINISH THE SOUP

1 Cut the red chilli lengthwise in half with the small knife. Cut out the core, scrape out the seeds, and cut away the fleshy white ribs. Set each chilli half cut-side up and thinly slice it lengthwise. Hold the strips together and cut across into very fine dice.

! TAKE CARE !
Wear rubber gloves when preparing chillies because they can burn your skin.

2 Heat the grill. Grate the cheese using the coarsest grid of the grater.

3 Spread the tortilla chips in a single layer on the baking sheet. Scatter the grated cheese over the chips, then sprinkle them with the diced chilli. Grill the chips close to the heat until the cheese has melted and is bubbly, 1–2 minutes. Keep the chips warm.

Chillies are hot so be sure to sprinkle them evenly over tortilla chips

Try not to get cheese on baking sheet or it will stick

VARIATION
CHILLED AVOCADO SOUP
The subtle taste of avocado comes to the fore in this simple yet elegant soup.

4 Stir three-quarters of the diced tomatoes and chopped coriander into the soup. If the soup seems too thick, add a little more stock, then taste the soup again for seasoning.

ANNE SAYS
"Tomatoes and coriander are added to the soup at the last moment so their flavours remain fresh."

⦿ TO SERVE
Ladle the soup into chilled bowls, garnish with the remaining tomato and coriander, and serve with the warm cheese-chilli tortilla chips.

1 Omit the limes, tequila, Tabasco sauce, tomatoes, and fresh coriander. Squeeze the juice from 1½ lemons; there should be 60 ml (4 tbsp) juice.
2 Cut 3 large avocados (total weight about 750 g/1½ lb) in half and remove the stones as directed.

3 Tightly wrap 1 avocado half and reserve. Scoop the flesh from the remaining avocado halves and put it into a large non-metallic bowl.
4 Add 375 ml (12 fl oz) cold chicken stock and 30 ml (2 tbsp) lemon juice to the avocado and purée as directed.
5 Add 125 ml (4 fl oz) medium-dry white wine, 250 ml (8 fl oz) soured cream, 5 ml (1 tsp) Worcestershire sauce, salt, and pepper. Purée again briefly to mix. Taste the soup for seasoning, adding more lemon juice, salt, and pepper if needed.
6 Cover the soup tightly and chill, at least 1 hour. Cut the reserved avocado half into quarters and strip off the skin. Cut each quarter into lengthwise slices. Cut the slices into strips, then cut them across into neat dice.
7 Stir the soup and add a little more stock if it seems too thick. Taste again for seasoning. Ladle the soup into chilled soup plates and garnish with the avocado dice. Cheese biscuits make a good accompaniment.

Chopped tomato adds texture to smooth guacamole soup

GAZPACHO

🍴 SERVES 4–6 🥣 WORK TIME 45–50 MINUTES*

EQUIPMENT

slotted spoon

chef's knife

small knife

food processor †

pastry brush

vegetable peeler

wooden spoon

saucepan

bowls

serrated knife

rubber spatula

baking sheet

chopping board

† blender can also be used

This iced soup, based on a purée of vegetables and fruity wine, originated in the hot climate of southern Spain. Make gazpacho in the summer and early autumn, when tomatoes and peppers are full of flavour.

GETTING AHEAD

The soup and croûtons can be made up to 1 day ahead. Keep the soup, covered, in the refrigerator, and the croûtons in an airtight container. Add the garnish just before serving.

* plus at least 1 hour chilling time

metric	SHOPPING LIST	imperial
2	slices of white bread	2
175 ml	tomato juice	6 fl oz
60 ml	fruity red wine	4 tbsp
750 g	ripe plum tomatoes	1½ lb
4	spring onions	4
1	large cucumber	1
1	red pepper	1
2	garlic cloves	2
45 ml	olive oil	3 tbsp
30 ml	red wine vinegar	2 tbsp
	salt and pepper	
	ice cubes (optional)	
	For the croûtons	
3	slices of white bread	3
45 ml	olive oil	3 tbsp

INGREDIENTS

tomato juice

red pepper

white bread

spring onions

fruity red wine

garlic cloves

red wine vinegar

plum tomatoes †

cucumber

olive oil

† medium tomatoes can also be used

ANNE SAYS
"A fruity red wine from southern Spain is the perfect choice when serving gazpacho."

ORDER OF WORK

1 PREPARE THE INGREDIENTS

2 MAKE AND CHILL THE SOUP

3 MAKE THE CROUTONS; FINISH THE SOUP

1 PREPARE THE INGREDIENTS

3 Trim the spring onions, leaving on most of the green tops. Using the chef's knife, slice the onions lengthwise in half, then cut them across into rough dice.

1 Using the serrated knife, trim and discard the crusts from the 2 slices of white bread. Roughly tear the slices of bread into pieces and place them in a small bowl.

2 Pour the tomato juice and red wine over the bread and set aside to soak. Peel, seed, and chop the tomatoes (see box, below). Reserve 45–60 ml (3–4 tbsp) tomatoes for garnish.

Spring onions are roughly chopped before puréeing in food processor

HOW TO PEEL, SEED, AND CHOP TOMATOES

Tomatoes are often peeled and seeded before they are chopped, so they form a smooth purée. The technique is the same for any variety of tomato.

1 Cut the cores from the tomatoes and score an "x" on the base of each tomato with the tip of a small knife.

2 Immerse the tomatoes in a pan of boiling water until the skins start to split, 8–15 seconds depending on their ripeness. Using a slotted spoon, transfer the tomatoes at once to a bowl of cold water.

3 When the tomatoes are cool enough to handle, peel the skin off each one, using the small knife.

4 With a chef's knife, cut the tomatoes crosswise in half. Squeeze out the seeds, then coarsely chop each tomato half.

Hold tip of blade and rock handle up and down

4 With the vegetable peeler, peel the cucumber. Cut it lengthwise in half and scrape out the seeds.

5 Slice each half of the cucumber lengthwise into strips, then gather the strips together and cut across into small dice. Reserve 45–60 ml (3–4 tbsp) dice for garnish.

Inside of red pepper is scraped clean of seeds and white ribs

6 Cut around the red pepper core, twist it out, and discard. Halve the pepper; scrape out the seeds and white ribs. Set one half, cut-side down, on the board, flatten, and slice lengthwise into strips. Gather the strips together and cut into dice. Repeat with the remaining pepper half, making finer dice. Reserve the finer dice for garnish.

Red pepper is diced so it is easy to work in processor

7 Set the flat side of the chef's knife on top of each garlic clove and strike it with your fist. Discard the skin and roughly chop the garlic.

2 MAKE AND CHILL THE SOUP

1 Put the soaked bread mixture into the food processor and add the tomatoes, spring onions, cucumber, garlic, and red pepper. Purée until smooth.

ANNE SAYS
"You will probably have to purée the mixture in 2–3 batches."

Garlic is roughly chopped before puréeing, so it will flavour soup evenly

Red pepper adds natural sweetness to soup

2 Transfer the puréed mixture to a large bowl and stir in the olive oil, vinegar, salt, and pepper. Cover, and chill thoroughly, at least 1 hour. Meanwhile, make the croûtons.

3 MAKE THE CROUTONS; FINISH THE SOUP

1 Heat the oven to 190°C (375°F, Gas 5). Trim and discard the crusts from the 3 slices of bread. Lightly brush the slices on both sides with the olive oil.

Olive oil flavours croûtons and makes them crunchy when cooked

Bread is brushed with oil before cutting into cubes to save time

2 Cut each slice of bread into 1 cm (³/₈ inch) strips, then gather the strips together and cut across to make cubes. Spread out the cubes on the baking sheet. Bake until the croûtons are golden brown and crisp, about 10 minutes. Stir halfway through baking so they brown evenly. Let cool.

🍴 TO SERVE

Stir the soup and taste for seasoning. If it is too thick, stir in some ice water. Pour into chilled serving bowls. Add 1–2 ice cubes, if you like. Garnish with the reserved vegetable dice and some of the croûtons. Serve the remaining croûtons separately.

Garnish hints at the flavourings in soup

V A R I A T I O N

GREEN GAZPACHO WITH CRAB

Here, gazpacho is made with green vegetables – a vivid background for the crabmeat and garnish of black olives.

1 Omit the tomato juice, red wine, tomatoes, and croûtons. Soak bread in 250 ml (8 fl oz) dry white wine.
2 Prepare the spring onions, cucumber, and garlic as directed; only peel the cucumber if the skin is waxed. Use 2 green peppers instead of 1 red; do not reserve any for garnish.
3 Strip the leaves from 3 sprigs each of coriander and flat-leaf parsley, reserving 4–6 tiny sprigs for garnish.
4 Put the prepared vegetables, herb leaves, and soaked bread mixture into a food processor or blender and work until the vegetables are finely chopped.
5 Transfer to a bowl and stir in 60 ml (4 tbsp) olive oil, juice of 1 lime, 30 ml (2 tbsp) rice vinegar, salt, and pepper. Cover, and chill, at least 1 hour.
6 Pick over 250 g (8 oz) cooked fresh or canned white crabmeat to remove any cartilage or shell. Coarsely flake the crabmeat with a fork.
7 Finely chop 4–5 pitted black olives and reserve for garnish.
8 Stir the soup well and taste for seasoning, adding more lime juice, rice vinegar, salt, and pepper if needed.
9 Ladle the soup into chilled bowls; add 1–2 ice cubes to each one. Divide the crabmeat among the bowls and garnish with herbs and black olives.

ICED CUCUMBER SOUP WITH YOGURT AND MINT

¶Ⓞ¶ SERVES 4–6   ⌣ WORK TIME 25–30 MINUTES*

EQUIPMENT

ladle

chef's knife

pastry brush

food processor †

bowls

saucepan

rubber spatula

baking sheet

chopping board

†hand or standard blender can also be used

Based on the Turkish salad cacik, *this refreshing chilled soup is ideal hot weather fare. The garnish of fresh mint frozen in cubes of ice adds a particularly cooling touch.*

GETTING AHEAD

The soup and the mint ice cubes can be made up to 2 days ahead. Keep the soup, covered, in the refrigerator and store the ice cubes in a plastic bag in the freezer.

* plus freezing time for mint ice cubes, and at least 1 hour chilling time for soup

metric	SHOPPING LIST	imperial
6	sprigs of fresh mint	6
500 g	cucumbers	1 lb
6	spring onions	6
250 ml	cold chicken stock (see box, page 125), more if needed	8 fl oz
250 ml	plain yogurt	8 fl oz
125 ml	soured cream	4 fl oz
	juice of 1 lemon	
	salt and pepper	
	For the garlic pita toasts	
2	garlic cloves	2
30–45 ml	olive oil	2–3 tbsp
3	oval pita breads	3

INGREDIENTS

fresh mint

garlic cloves

cucumbers

lemon juice

olive oil

soured cream

chicken stock

spring onions

pita breads

plain yogurt

ANNE SAYS

"Try to find cucumbers with unwaxed skins, otherwise you will have to peel them and the soup will be very pale."

ORDER OF WORK

1 MAKE THE MINT ICE CUBES

2 MAKE AND CHILL THE SOUP

3 MAKE THE GARLIC PITA TOASTS

1 MAKE THE MINT ICE CUBES

Choose small
bright leaves
for ice cubes

1 Boil some water and let it cool in
the saucepan. Strip the mint leaves
from the stalks.

2 Half fill each compartment of an
ice-cube tray with the cooled boiled
water. Select small leaves or tiny top
sprigs of mint and put one in each
compartment, pushing it down into the
water. Freeze until solid. Reserve the
remaining mint leaves.

Boiled water
makes clear
ice cubes

3 Add more cooled boiled water to
the ice-cube tray to fill the
compartments. Return to the freezer.

2 MAKE AND CHILL THE SOUP

1 Trim the ends off the cucumbers
with the chef's knife, then slice
them lengthwise in half. Scoop out the
seeds with a teaspoon and discard
them. Slice each cucumber half
lengthwise into strips, then
gather the strips together and
cut across into dice.

ANNE SAYS
"*If the cucumber skins are
waxed, peel them with a
vegetable peeler.*"

Cucumber skin
adds colour to soup

Dicing with chef's
knife is quick
and efficient

2 Using the chef's knife, trim the
spring onions and coarsely chop
them, including their green tops.

Green tops of spring
onions have milder
flavour than
white bulbs

3 Pile the remaining mint leaves on
the chopping board and finely chop
them with the chef's knife.

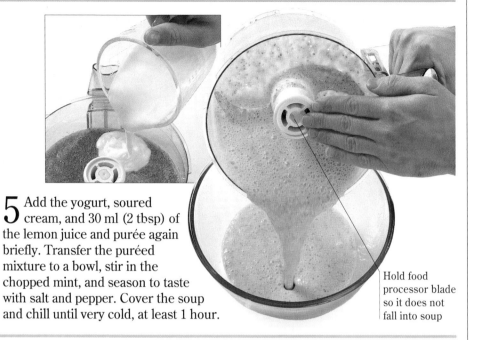

4 Put the cucumber and spring onions in the food processor, add the cold chicken stock, and purée until smooth. Alternatively, purée the soup with a hand or standard blender.

5 Add the yogurt, soured cream, and 30 ml (2 tbsp) of the lemon juice and purée again briefly. Transfer the puréed mixture to a bowl, stir in the chopped mint, and season to taste with salt and pepper. Cover the soup and chill until very cold, at least 1 hour.

Hold food processor blade so it does not fall into soup

3 MAKE THE GARLIC PITA TOASTS

1 Finely chop the garlic (see box, page 117). Combine the olive oil and garlic in a small bowl.

2 Heat the oven to 220° C (Gas 7, 425° F). Cut each pita bread crosswise in half, then into quarters, on the diagonal. Trim and discard all the long rounded edges from the pita triangles.

3 Open up and separate the triangles. Each pita bread will make 8 triangles.

Split pita breads crisp when baked

Wholemeal pita breads are used here, but plain ones can also be used

4 Brush the inside of the bread with the garlic oil and place, oiled-side up, on the baking sheet. Season with salt and pepper. Bake in the heated oven until crisp and lightly browned, 8–10 minutes.

HOW TO PEEL AND CHOP GARLIC

The strength of garlic varies with its age and dryness; use more when it is very fresh.

1 To peel a garlic clove, lightly crush it with the flat side of a chef's knife to loosen the skin.

2 Peel the skin from the garlic clove with your fingers and discard. Set the flat side of the chef's knife on top and strike it firmly with your fist.

Rocking action speeds chopping

3 Finely chop the garlic clove with the chef's knife, rocking the blade back and forth.

🍽 TO SERVE

Stir the soup well and add more stock if it is too thick. Taste for seasoning, adding more lemon juice, salt, and pepper if needed. Ladle into chilled bowls, adding ice cubes to each one. Serve the garlic pita toasts separately.

Ice cubes studded with mint leaves decorate and chill soup

VARIATION

CHILLED SPINACH AND YOGURT SOUP

A garlicky spinach purée is mixed with yogurt and soured cream to make this unusual chilled soup.

1 Omit the cucumbers and mint ice cubes. Strip the leaves from 3 sprigs of fresh mint and finely chop them.
2 Prepare the spring onions as directed; chop them finely. Chop the garlic. Discard the ribs and stalks from 500 g (1 lb) spinach. Wash the leaves.
3 Heat 30 ml (2 tbsp) vegetable oil in a frying pan, sauté the spring onions, garlic, and spinach, stirring, until wilted, 3–4 minutes. Add the chicken stock, salt, and pepper and bring to a boil. Simmer, stirring occasionally, about 10 minutes.
4 Let the soup cool slightly, then purée it in a food processor. Transfer to a bowl and let cool.
5 Cut 1 lemon in half. Squeeze the juice from one half. Thinly slice the other half and make lemon twists: cut from centre to edge of each slice, then twist the cut edges in opposite directions.
6 Stir in the yogurt, soured cream, mint, lemon juice, salt, and pepper. Cover and chill, at least 3 hours.
7 Taste the soup for seasoning, ladle into chilled soup plates, and decorate each one with a lemon twist.

CHILLED HUNGARIAN CHERRY SOUP

†⦿¶ SERVES 4–6 ⇔ WORK TIME 30 MINUTES* ♨ COOKING TIME 5–10 MINUTES

EQUIPMENT

cherry stoner†

chef's knife

blender‡

metal spoon

lemon squeezer

small sieve

wooden spoon

large sieve

bowls

saucepans

INGREDIENTS

cherries†

buttermilk‡

sugar

fruity white wine

double cream

kirsch

lemons

†two 500 g (1 lb) cans cherries, well-drained, can also be used

‡soured cream and 2.5 ml (½ tsp) lemon juice can also be used

ANNE SAYS
"*You can substitute 750 ml (1¼ pints) shop-bought crème fraîche for the homemade version used in this recipe.*"

Fruit soups are a great favourite in eastern Europe and Scandinavia, and they deserve to be much more widely known. This cherry soup is creamy, with a pleasant fruity tartness, backed by a subtle hint of spice. Made with Bing or other dark sweet cherries, it makes a refreshing start to any meal and doubles as a summer dessert if you add a little more sugar.

GETTING AHEAD

The soup can be made up to 1 day ahead and kept, covered, in the refrigerator. Just before serving, stir it well and then add the decoration.

* plus 6–8 hours for making crème fraîche and at least 2 hours for chilling soup

metric	SHOPPING LIST	imperial
500 g	dark sweet cherries	1 lb
100 g	sugar, more if needed	3½ oz
750 ml	fruity white wine, such as a Riesling (1 bottle)	1¼ pints
2	lemons	2
30 ml	kirsch	2 tbsp
	ground cinnamon for sprinkling (optional)	
	For the crème fraîche	
500 ml	double cream	16 fl oz
250 ml	live culture buttermilk	8 fl oz

†vegetable peeler can also be used

‡food processor can also be used

ORDER OF WORK

1 MAKE THE CREME FRAICHE

2 PREPARE AND POACH THE CHERRIES

3 FINISH AND CHILL THE SOUP

1 MAKE THE CREME FRAICHE

1 Pour the double cream into a medium saucepan, add the buttermilk, and stir to mix. Heat gently until the cream feels just barely warm (about 24°C/75°F). Pour the mixture into a glass bowl or measuring jug.

ANNE SAYS
"*Be sure the buttermilk specifies 'live culture' on the label.*"

2 Cover, leaving a gap for air. Leave at room temperature (21°C/70°F) until the cream has thickened enough to hold the mark of a spoon and tastes slightly acidic, 6–8 hours. Stir, cover, and chill.

2 PREPARE AND POACH THE CHERRIES

1 Discard any cherry stalks. Using the cherry stoner, remove the stones from the cherries. If using a vegetable peeler, insert the tip of the peeler in the stalk end of the cherry, rotate around the stone, and scoop it out.

ANNE SAYS
"*A cherry stoner is a convenient tool because it pushes the stone through the fruit, leaving a hollow centre. As a result, more of the cherry juices are released when the cherries are cooked.*"

Cherries are stoned quickly with cherry stoner

2 Put the cherries into a medium saucepan. Add the sugar and wine, and heat, stirring occasionally, until the sugar has dissolved.

ANNE SAYS
"*Use a non-aluminium saucepan because the acid in the cherries and wine can react with aluminium to give a metallic taste.*"

3 Bring to a boil and simmer, stirring occasionally, until the cherries are soft, 3–5 minutes. Let cool slightly.

Cherries simmer briefly in fruity white wine

3 FINISH AND CHILL THE SOUP

Strain lemon
juice to catch
pips

After blending, cherry
purée should be smooth
pouring consistency

1 Cut the lemons
in half and squeeze the
juice with the lemon squeezer. Strain
the juice into a measuring jug; there
should be 90 ml (3 fl oz) juice.

2 Pour the cooled
cherry mixture
into the blender or food processor.
Purée the mixture until it is smooth,
in 2–3 batches if necessary.

4 Stir the kirsch and three-quarters
of the crème fraîche into the soup
until evenly mixed.

Colour of cherry
soup will lighten
with addition of
crème fraîche

Crème fraîche
thickens cherry
mixture

3 Using the back of a metal spoon,
press the cherry purée through the
sieve set over a large bowl. Stir in the
lemon juice.

ANNE SAYS
"*Pressure from the back of the spoon
pushes the cherry purée through the
sieve efficiently.*"

CHILLED RASPBERRY AND PEACH SOUP

Raspberries and peaches give fruity sweetness to this wine-based soup. Serve the soup as soon as possible after making, otherwise the fruit may deteriorate.

5 Taste the soup and add more sugar if needed. Cover, and chill thoroughly, at least 2 hours.

¶●¶ TO SERVE

Stir the soup well, then pour into a chilled bowl or tureen. Ladle into chilled individual bowls and swirl a little of the remaining crème fraîche on each one. If you like, sprinkle with a little cinnamon. Serve immediately.

1 Omit the crème fraîche, cherries, kirsch, and cinnamon. In a large saucepan, combine the juice from 1 orange and 1 lemon with 30 ml (2 tbsp) sugar. Cook over low heat, stirring, until the sugar dissolves, 2–3 minutes. Remove from the heat.

2 Peel 375 g (12 oz) ripe peaches: immerse in boiling water, 10 seconds, and immediately transfer to cold water. Cut each peach in half, using the indentation on one side as a guide. Twist with both hands to loosen the halves, then pull them apart. Remove the stone and peel the skin. Cut each half into slices, dropping them at once into the citrus syrup so they do not discolour. Cook the peaches over low heat, stirring, until tender, 3–5 minutes. Let cool, then stir in 500 g (1 lb) fresh or drained defrosted raspberries, reserving some for garnish.

3 Transfer the raspberry and peach mixture to a blender or food processor and purée until smooth. Work the purée through a sieve set over a bowl to remove the raspberry seeds.

4 Add 500 ml (16 fl oz) medium-dry white wine and stir well to mix. Taste the soup, and add more orange juice, lemon juice, and sugar if needed.

5 Cover, and chill thoroughly, at least 2 hours. Serve the soup within 6 hours.

6 Divide the soup among 4–6 chilled individual soup bowls. Lightly whip 125 ml (4 fl oz) double cream and add a generous spoonful to each serving. Top each one with some of the reserved raspberries.

Swirl of crème fraîche is a simple but pretty decoration

Soft pretty pink of soup is enhanced by glass bowl

SOUPS KNOW-HOW

The role of soup in a meal changes according to the type and style of the meal, and to the time of year – refreshing cold soups on hot days, warming rich soups in the depths of winter. The components of a soup can be decided by a particular recipe for a certain occasion, by what is in season, or by what is on hand in the cupboard and refrigerator. Finance plays its part too – soup has always been the economical option for feeding a hungry family.

makes a more substantial meal. A few suggestions are Thai Hot and Sour Prawn Soup followed by a crunchy vegetable salad, Turkish Meatball Soup with pita bread, Spiced Carrot and Parsnip Soup with a ham sandwich, Cheddar and Vegetable Soup with dark rye or wholemeal bread, or Gazpacho with cheese and fruit.

The hearty soups in this book are unashamedly main courses. Their protein content – from meat, fish, poultry, or vegetables – and their carbohydrate content is enough to satisfy the hungriest of eaters, making these soups almost meals in themselves, although bread or rice and a crisp salad are always welcome accompaniments. Nor are all these main-course soups everyday fare – a well-made Gumbo, or the Monkfish and Garlic Soup with Saffron, is certainly worthy of a special occasion.

CHOOSING SOUPS

The clear, creamed, and cold soups in this book are ideal as first courses, and there are recipes here to suit all kinds of menus, whether they are elegant or everyday. Many can also be served alone for a light lunch or for supper with bread or scones, while the addition of a sandwich or a salad

SOUPS AND YOUR HEALTH

Today's health-conscious cooks are eager for recipes low in saturated fat and calories, and high in vegetables and carbohydrates. While all the soups in this volume have a place in a healthy diet, a few minor adjustments to those recipes containing high-fat ingredients can make them suitable for those who must pay special attention to particular dietary concerns.

Most recipes begin with a small quantity of butter or oil which may be adjusted to lighten the fat and calorie content of the soup. For butter, substitute monounsaturated olive oil or a highly unsaturated vegetable oil. Whatever fat is used, reduce the quantity slightly as well. Recipes calling for bacon, salt pork, or ham will be equally delicous, though lighter in flavour and body, when made without them. Be sure to adjust the quantity of added salt when eliminating a salty ingredient from a soup.

In some recipes, high-fat and cholesterol elements are an integral part of the soup – rich cream in Vichyssoise, for example. In these cases, I don't recommend substituting ingredients, but rather serving these soups as special-occasion treats. After all, pleasure at the dinner table is key to a healthy lifestyle, too!

GETTING AHEAD

Soup is a boon to a busy cook because it can often be made whenever convenient and then refrigerated, to be reheated (or kept chilled) and finished at the last minute. Some soups, such as French Onion Soup, German Split Pea Soup, Chicken and Smoked Ham Gumbo, and Gazpacho, even improve on being kept a day or two because their flavour mellows. Only those soups with perishable or lightly cooked ingredients must be made just before serving, and even they will usually permit some advance preparation. Examples here include Turkish Meatball Soup, where the meatballs and vegetables can be prepared 8 hours ahead, and Red Pepper Soup with Coriander Pesto – both soup and pesto can be made the day before and kept separately.

PRESENTING SOUPS

The visual impact of a soup has much to do with its enjoyment, so the container in which it is served is important to the overall appeal of the dish. Chunky soups, full of diced vegetables, meat, and pasta, look good in deep soup bowls or ladled from a tureen. If the soup is a rustic or hearty one, a thick pottery or glazed earthenware bowl will suit it well, whereas puréed soups such as Peppery Green Soup or Butternut Squash and Apple Soup need lighter, more traditional soup bowls and plates or tureens. In clear soups, decorative vegetables, stuffed wontons, or pasta are all the decoration needed, so the bowl should be completely plain. Soups with considerably more liquid than solid ingredients are best presented in wide, shallow soup plates, while creamed and clear soups look grand in two-handled china soup cups set on saucers or plates.

These cups are good for cold soups too, as are glass bowls chilled in the refrigerator, or even bowls set in slightly larger ones containing crushed ice.

The garnishing or decoration of a soup is the final, vital part of its presentation. This can range from a simple swirl of cream, a sprinkling of herbs, or a little cluster of vegetable julienne to a dramatic and stylish pattern made with a sauce of a contrasting colour. Some garnishes add complementary textures and flavours: toasted nuts, crisp bacon, slices of hard-boiled egg. Crunchy croûtons and toasted bread croûtes topped with cheese are traditional garnishes for soup as well. Accompany creamed and puréed soups with small, crispy croûtons that will stay crisp in the soup. You can use bigger croûtons, or croûtes, if you like, to garnish clear broths. Clear soups soak the croûte so it becomes tender enough to cut into with a soup spoon. Whatever the finishing touch, it should contrast with the appearance, and highlight the texture and flavour of the soup itself.

MICROWAVE

While the traditional image of homemade soup includes a long-simmering stockpot bubbling on the back of the stove, the speed of the microwave oven can also be put to good use when making soups.

Certain basic preparations may be speeded up slightly by using the microwave, however a more general use is for defrosting frozen stocks and soups. Large batches of basic stocks can be made when you have time to spare, divided into smaller microwave-safe freezer containers, and frozen until ready to use. Simply pop the container into the microwave and thaw. (Fill containers by only two-thirds so the liquid can expand during freezing, and so it doesn't boil over during reheating.) The same goes for finished soups. Make a full – or even a double – batch of your favourite recipe to freeze in usable quantities so you have a supply when you need a meal in a hurry – for unexpected guests, a late-night snack, or simply after a hard day's work.

When heating any soup in the microwave, be sure to stir occasionally, and especially just before you serve it, so no "hot spots" remain.

HOW-TO BOXES

In each of the recipes in **Splendid Soups**, *you will find pictures of all the techniques used. However, some basic preparations appear in a number of recipes, and these are shown in extra detail in these special "how-to" boxes:*

BEEF STOCK

Beef stock is based on raw meat bones gently simmered with aromatic vegetables in water and can be refrigerated for up to 3 days. If you are keeping it longer, reheat it and simmer on top of the stove, about 10 minutes. Let cool, and refrigerate again.

🍴 MAKES 2–3 LITRES (3½ –5 PINTS)

🥣 WORK TIME 20–30 MINUTES

🍲 COOKING TIME 4–5 HOURS

SHOPPING LIST

2 kg	beef bones, cut into pieces	4½ lb
2	onions	2
2	carrots	2
2	celery sticks	2
4 litres	water, more if needed	7 pints
1	bouquet garni	1
10	black peppercorns	10
1	garlic clove	1
15 ml	tomato purée	1 tbsp

1 Heat the oven to 230°C (450°F, Gas 8). Put the bones into a large roasting tin and roast until they are well browned, stirring occasionally, about 40 minutes. Peel and quarter the onions and carrots. Quarter the celery. Add the vegetables to the tin and roast until brown, stirring occasionally, 15–20 minutes.

2 With a slotted spoon, transfer the bones and vegetables to a large saucepan. Discard the fat from the roasting tin and add 500 ml (16 fl oz) of the water. Bring to a boil, stirring to dissolve the pan juices.

3 Add the liquid to the pan with all the remaining ingredients, then add enough water just to cover the bones. Bring slowly to a boil, skimming often. As soon as the liquid comes to a boil, lower the heat and simmer gently, uncovered, skimming occasionally, 4–5 hours. Add more water, if needed, to keep the bones covered.

4 Strain the stock, then taste it. If the flavour is not strong enough, boil the stock to reduce until concentrated. Remove from the heat, let cool, then chill. When cold, the fat will be solid and easy to discard.

VEGETABLE STOCK

Vegetable stock is an excellent, light alternative to meat or chicken stock in many recipes. You can use it to transform some meat recipes into vegetarian ones. It can be refrigerated for up to 3 days, though it will lose some of its fresh flavour.

🍴 MAKES 1.5 LITRES (2 PINTS)

🥣 WORK TIME 15 MINUTES

🍲 COOKING TIME 1 HOUR

SHOPPING LIST

3	onions	3
3–4	carrots	3–4
3	celery sticks	3
2	garlic cloves (optional)	2
2 litres	water, more if needed	3½ pints
1	bouquet garni	1
10	black peppercorns	10

1 Peel the onions, leaving a little of the roots attached, and cut them lengthwise in half. Lay each half cut-side down on a chopping board and chop it coarsely.

2 Peel the carrots and trim off the ends. Cut each carrot into 7.5 cm (3 inch) pieces. Cut each piece lengthwise into 5 mm (¼ inch) slices. Stack the slices and cut each stack into 4–6 strips. Gather the strips together in a pile and cut across to form medium dice.

3 Cut the celery stalks across into 7.5 cm (3 inch) pieces, then cut each piece lengthwise in half. Stack the halves and cut across to form medium dice.

4 If using garlic, set the flat side of the chef's knife on top of the garlic clove and strike it firmly with your fist. Discard the skin.

5 Put the vegetables into a large saucepan and add the water, bouquet garni, and peppercorns. Bring slowly to a boil, and simmer, uncovered, 1 hour. Skim the stock occasionally with a large metal spoon.

6 Remove from the heat. Strain the stock into a bowl. Let cool, then cover, and keep in the refrigerator.

CHICKEN STOCK

Chicken stock is an indispensable ingredient in many soup recipes. It keeps well for up to 3 days, covered, in the refrigerator and can be reboiled for longer storage (see Beef Stock, page 124). Chicken stock also freezes well.

🍽 MAKES ABOUT 2 LITRES (3¼ PINTS)

🥣 WORK TIME 15 MINUTES

🍲 COOKING TIME UP TO 3 HOURS

SHOPPING LIST

1 kg	raw chicken backs and necks	2 lb
1	onion	1
1	carrot	1
1	celery stick	1
1	bouquet garni	1
5	black peppercorns	5
2 litres	water, more if needed	3¼ pints

1 Put the chicken into a large pan. Peel and quarter the onion. Quarter the carrot and celery stick. Add to the pan with the bouquet garni and peppercorns.

2 Add water just to cover the ingredients. Bring slowly to a boil, and simmer, skimming occasionally with a large metal spoon, up to 3 hours. Add more water if necessary to keep the ingredients covered.

ANNE SAYS
"To freeze stock, boil it until concentrated, then freeze in ice-cube trays for convenience."

3 Strain the stock into a large bowl. Cool, then cover, and keep in the refrigerator.

ANNE SAYS
"The longer the chicken stock is simmered, the more flavour it will have."

FISH STOCK

Bones, heads, and tails of lean white fish, especially flatfish such as sole, are recommended for stock. Avoid oily fish, such as mackerel. Fish stock keeps well for up to 2 days, covered, in the refrigerator, or it can be frozen.

🍽 MAKES ABOUT 1 LITRE (1⅔ PINTS)

🥣 WORK TIME 10–15 MINUTES

🍲 COOKING TIME 20 MINUTES

SHOPPING LIST

750 g	fish bones and heads	1½ lb
1	onion	1
250 ml	dry white wine or juice of ½ lemon	8 fl oz
1 litre	water, more if needed	1⅔ pints
3–5	sprigs of parsley	3–5
5 ml	peppercorns	1 tsp

1 Thoroughly wash the fish bones and heads. Cut the bones into 4–5 pieces with a chef's knife. Peel the onion, leaving a little of the root attached, then cut it lengthwise in half. Lay each onion half flat on a chopping board and cut across into thin slices.

2 Put the fish bones and heads into a medium pan with the onion slices, wine or lemon juice, water, parsley sprigs, and peppercorns. Bring slowly to a boil and simmer, 20 minutes. Skim the stock occasionally with a large metal spoon.

! TAKE CARE !
Do not simmer fish stock too long or it will be bitter.

3 Strain the stock into a bowl. Let cool, then cover, and keep in the refrigerator.

ANNE SAYS
"I never season stock with salt and ground pepper at the time of making, because it may be reduced later in individual recipes and the flavours will intensify."

INDEX

ACKNOWLEDGMENTS

Photographers David Murray
Jules Selmes
Photographer's Assistant Steve Head
Photography Art Direction Vicky Zentner

Chef Eric Treuille
Cookery Consultant Martha Holmberg
Home Economist Sarah Lowman

Reader Lisa Minsky
Indexer Julia Alcock

Typesetting Linda Parker
Text film by Disc to Print (UK) Limited

Production Consultant Lorraine Baird

Carroll & Brown Limited would like to thank ICTC (081 568-4179) for supplying the Cuisinox Elysee pans used throughout the book, Magimix (UK) Limited who supplied the Cuisine Systeme food processor, and Corning Limited who supplied the Pyrex cookware.

Anne Willan wishes to thank writer Norma MacMillan and the staff at Carroll & Brown in London for their vital help in writing this book and testing the recipes, aided by La Varenne's editors and trainees.

NOTES

- Metric and imperial measures have been calculated separately. Only use one set of measures as they are not exact equivalents.

- All spoon measurements are level.

- Spoon measurements are calculated using a standard 5 ml teaspoon and 15 ml tablespoon to give an accurate measurement of small amounts.